THE BOOK OF
JUDITH

Jack and Masks. Credit: Jim Carlson.

THE BOOK OF
JUDITH

Opening Hearts Through Poetry

Edited by

Sara Press

Mark Foss

Spoon Jackson

New Village Press ★ New York

Published in the United States by New Village Press
bookorders@newvillagepress.net
www.newvillagepress.org

New Village Press is a public-benefit, nonprofit publisher
Distributed by NYU Press

Publication Date: September 13, 2022
First Edition

Library of Congress Cataloging-in-Publication Data

Names: Press, Sara, editor. | Foss, Mark, editor. | Jackson, Spoon, editor.
Title: The book of Judith : opening hearts through poetry / edited by Spoon Jackson, Mark Foss, and Sara Press.
Description: First edition. | New York : New Village Press, 2022. | Includes bibliographical references. | Summary: "An homage to the life of poet, writer, and teaching artist Judith Tannenbaum (b. 1947 – d. 2019) and her impact on incarcerated and marginalized students. The book presents different aspects of Judith through a collection of original poetry, prose, essay, illustration, and fiction from 33 contributors who knew her." —Provided by publisher.
Identifiers: LCCN 2021062323 (print) | LCCN 2021062324 (ebook) | ISBN 9781613321751 (hardcover) | ISBN 9781613321744 (paperback) | ISBN 9781613321768 (ebook) | ISBN 9781613321775 (international ebook)
Subjects: LCSH: Tannenbaum, Judith. | Tannenbaum, Judith--Anecdotes. | Women poets, American—Biography. | English teachers—United States—Biography. | Poetry—Study and teaching—United States. | Prisoners—Education--United States. | Elegiac poetry, American.
Classification: LCC PS3620.A6865 Z58 2022 (print) | LCC PS3620.A6865 (ebook) | LCC 811/.54—dc23/eng/20220314
LC record available at https://lccn.loc.gov/2021062323
LC ebook record available at https://lccn.loc.gov/2021062324

Cover design: Lynne Elizabeth
Cover and author photo: Rainer Komers
Text design and composition: Leigh McLellan Design

Contents

Contents

After December 61

Looking and Listening 75

Legacy 125

Preface

MY MOTHER, Judith Tannenbaum, once said that at least half her poems were prayers. As a middle schooler, helping her learn poems by heart so she could recite them at readings, I didn't understand their depth. Now I do, and as I discovered through this book, I'm not alone.

Born in 1947, my mom published her first poem at the age of nineteen, and went on to publish many more. Apart from poetry, she wrote multiple books, ranging from memoirs and novels to essays and teaching texts.

My mom was also a teacher, and later a teaching artist. She began teaching writing and literature classes in 1970 in Berkeley, California. She continued when we lived on the rural south coast of Mendocino County, and then in Albany and El Cerrito. Over the years, she taught in public schools, community centers, art centers, through California Poets in the Schools, Santa Rosa Junior College, the University of California at Berkeley, and in prisons and juvenile facilities.

For twenty years, she was a faculty member, primarily as training coordinator, of WritersCorps, a project of the San Francisco Arts Commission. There she was able to dive deep, which was her preferred approach, and guide teachers and students in being observant and honest. She also sat on workshop panels and spoke at conferences throughout the country, where she shared her vision and experiences at the intersection of prison, art, and social justice.

I was in high school when my mom taught poetry at San Quentin State Prison, on the northwest shore of San Francisco Bay. This was a turning point for her. As she put it in her memoir of those years: "During my years at the prison, I watched these men live their lives behind locked gates and cell bars; what I witnessed, as well as what I myself experienced, taught me as much about what it is to be a human being as I taught my students about poetry."[1]

I remember her getting home late on Monday evenings from teaching at San Quentin and needing to share some intense story about the day, even if I was half asleep in bed. Of course, now I wish I had listened more closely.

I first met Spoon Jackson, who was one of my mother's students, when he was performing in Samuel Beckett's play *Waiting for Godot* at San Quentin. I turned eighteen just in time to get permission to enter the prison, where my mother had been working hard to help bring this performance into being. Over the decades, their friendship deepened. She would share updates with me about Spoon's multiple endeavors, or I would be at her apartment when he called from prison.

My mom died on December 5, 2019. Soon thereafter, Spoon put out the call for a coeditor to help bring together his vision for *The Book of Judith,* and I was intrigued. I am not a professional writer or editor and didn't know a thing about publishing a book—although I had heard what a frustrating process it can be. But I wanted to see this book come to fruition, I wanted to work with Spoon, and I wanted to keep my mom as close as possible. Plus, I was an experienced project manager, which I figured would come in handy. How hard could it be to organize people's writings into a book? Little did I know!

I was also surprised, in a good way, by how much all the writings touched me. I appreciated being in contact with all the contributors, letting their condolences and reminiscences sink in. While I knew some well, others I knew only by their names. In both cases, reading everyone's writing helped me feel not so alone in my grief. As each friend and colleague shared his or her story or experience of my mother, I could see the influence she'd had on that person and thus on the world. I'm grateful that she had so many people and communities with which to share, with such integrity and love, how she saw the world. At the same time, I feel lucky that I got to be her daughter!

I am deeply appreciative of all the contributors for their stories, perspectives, thoughts, and lessons, which have created a beautiful multifaceted image of my mother and her journey. I will always be grateful to Spoon for his magic in engaging so many busy and wonderful people in this tribute. I send a big thank-you to Mark Foss, whose commitment, editing skills, and calm, kind manner made this book come to life. And another big thank-you to Lynne Elizabeth at New Village Press, who was behind this project from the start. Her enthusiasm, guidance, and encouragement have been instrumental in its success.

My mom, Judith Tannenbaum, lived how she wanted to—until her body gave out. She had a strong vision for her life and could only live true to herself. Writing was a fundamental component of this. She was driven to see both the light and dark, and to see the whole from the individual parts.

Toward the end, my mom urged me to keep my eyes and my heart open. This project was a way to do that.

S.P.

* * *

I never knew Judith Tannenbaum in life, but I came to know her indirectly through the journey of this book. Indeed, I have come to envy her friends, students, colleagues, and other loved ones for the time they had with this extraordinary woman. There is so much to appreciate and respect in Judith: her urge to create;

her iron will in the face of chronic pain and her empathy for the pain of others; the desire to share her passion for the arts, especially poetry, through teaching; her commitment to lifelong friendships; her curiosity, openness, and endless self-inquiry; her ability to hold space in a classroom so the most marginalized and at risk could find their voices. No wonder she evoked such intense loyalty. No wonder her passing has been such a devastating loss to all who knew and loved her, and to the Arts in Corrections community as a whole.

I came to this project through my friendship with Spoon Jackson, who is someone else I met indirectly. In 2013, I had worked on *Spoon,* a film by my partner, Michka Saäl. A poetic and political exchange imbedded on the dunes of the Mojave, *Spoon* explores whether writing poetry can erase steel bars, defy time, justify survival, and create space for inner freedom. Like many people who see the film, I was mesmerized by the force of Spoon's words, his voice, and his resilience.

After Michka passed away unexpectedly in 2017, Spoon and I met—through the written and spoken word—for the first time. Our ongoing contact consoles us both for the loss, I think. At screenings of *Spoon,* I read his greetings to the audience and tell them how he's doing. Yes, still in prison, still writing, still hoping for commutation. More than that, I cannot presume to understand.

When Spoon sent word to the outside that he needed an editor for *The Book of Judith,* I answered the call, reassured that Judith's daughter would be part of our collaboration. Drawing on an intimate knowledge of her mother's life, Sara reached out to potential contributors in Judith's network. In her review of the texts, she also gently corrected details that had gotten misremembered over the decades.

Our work began slowly in October 2020, just as the second wave of COVID-19 took hold. I had begun my journey of connecting with the diverse contributors to the book, and learning their stories. Meanwhile, the pandemic was sweeping through the prison system. When an inmate in his dorm fell sick, Spoon was moved to a single cell for protection against the pandemic. The virus found him all the same. It passed through steel, like words.

For a month, there was no news. His lawyer finally marshaled Spoon's vast network to flood the prison family hotline with messages. Only then did we learn Spoon was in a hospital outside the prison. He had pneumonia, and was breathing with help from a respirator. Then silence again.

Anyone who received a rare call from Spoon shared news on Facebook. The nurses were kind, he had told someone, and he was eating vegetables he had never tasted before in his life. But mostly we waited for news in silence, sending emails into the void and hoping they reached him. In "Empty Spaces," Spoon writes, "Sometimes the world doesn't/care what we think."

In February 2021, Spoon called from the prison hospital this time. Breathing and walking were still difficult. He rolled himself on a chair with casters to reach the telephone. His steely resolve to overcome adversity helped put the minor inconveniences of lockdown in Montreal into perspective. In "No World," Spoon writes, "If we aren't careful/our own little worlds/can become prisons."

As Spoon recovered over the next few months, I sent him emails of the contributions for his comments. I would make a list of points to discuss on his next call—whose piece had arrived, whose was delayed. Each time, he had already gotten the news from his network. More than that, I realized that his calls to people—all the encouraging and inspiring words—were the driving force behind everything.

The words of some poets and writers came easily. Others struggled, sometimes for months, to find the right way to express their deep feelings for Judith and her work. It was a privilege to be part of everyone's process.

M.F.

⋆ ⋆ ⋆

I know death is rising over the mountains, slowly, and the pain must be enormous. Yet Judith finds and creates beauty and peace even in the midst of a hurricane. She transforms in the middle of death. Judith has been dealing with great physical and mental pain all of her life, and yet she is like a birthing star, always growing and sending out and being love. I don't know what my world will be without her, hollow and empty.

But it's not about me, and I am sure she left some of her heart and spirit inside each of us—a shining light in darkness. Judith's curiosity and loyalty are unmatched even by goddesses or gods. If she believed in you, she inspired you to be yourself and change the world, if only the small world you knew. She lies there holding hands with Death, and yet no bitterness enters her heart, and joy fills her spirit. She has made everyone better by her presence and walk in this life, and Judith's love and magic live on in all of us who knew her and were and still are blessed by her.

⋆ ⋆ ⋆

After Judith passed, a lot of us who knew her made contact and had long conversations. One of those talks was with my "sister" Katie. I had known her for over twenty years but had never heard her voice. I suggested we should do a book about our Judith experiences. Katie agreed instantly, and so did Sara, Judith's daughter, and many others.

I believe, like Judith did, that death is a transformation of space, our bodies' being temporary homes. Judith's effects on different individuals were and are unique experiences that keep growing and giving. Even though physically she is gone,

Judith, for many, many months, prepared me and her daughter, Sara, for her transformation.

Long before she left, Judith asked some of my friends how to tell me about her death. In the end, her silence spoke novels—her silent love and silence on the phone told me and prepared me. Judith died, but she did not leave us. She meshed with each of us. I still hear her voice, see her smile, and feel her vibe, especially when I close my eyes.

Why write this book? Why believe in truth, magic, and the power of love? Why believe in trees and mountain paths?

Why write this book? Because I—because we—who knew Judith and loved her know her work is still being done. She is still with us, even advising me on this book and appreciating it in her humble ways. She is pleased we have shared this magic—these magic connections that unite, spread love, and give light. It tears me up to write about this.

Almost at the same time that I came up with the idea of writing this book, the title *The Book of Judith* was born. My idea was to try to keep that light alive—that orb of inspiration and insight Judith naturally shared with others.

I saw *The Book of Judith* as a testament to how real and powerful Judith still is. Because she has never left me. Such life and light Judith shared here and around the world never died and must be offered to others.

Judith, you left no one behind, because we all go with you and you with us! I love you, Big Sis.

S.J.

Unfinished Conversations

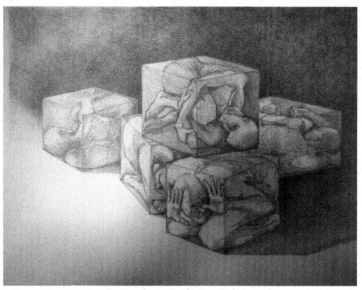

Box Study #1. Credit: Jim Carlson.

IN THE OPENING POEM, Judith Tannenbaum evokes light and love over two mugs of hot tea in her kitchen on a late California afternoon. The memory of such rituals comforts many of the contributors in this section. Some met with her each week, exchanging ideas about social justice work. Others met her in person only once or twice, sustaining their friendship through letters and phone calls. Several recollect their shared lives as kindred spirits. Others write imaginary letters, while still others share earlier exchanges connected to Judith. The final two pieces end with the same Jewish prayer.

In That Light

Judith Tannenbaum

Of course love rhymes with small roses
climbing a trellis above metal tracks,
crisscrossing slats that make diamond-shaped spaces,
flat strips of wood, light falling through.
And love in the hum of the train tracks themselves.
Engine, caboose, boxcar, and coach
pull into the station well after sunset, windows ablaze.
Isn't that love shining through the brightly lit glass?

As the light shone around Shandy as we sat at the table.
His red hair turning everything auburn:
kitchen curtain, books on white shelves,
wooden chairs, paisley cloth, two mugs of hot tea.
The air swirling reddish that California mid-summer late
    afternoon.
Light. Love. Love in that light.

True Colors

Allie Horevitz

In 2005, I was a twenty-two-year-old in my final semester at the University of Michigan, enrolled in one of the most talked-about classes among social justice–oriented students: English 319, "Theater and Social Change," with Professor Buzz Alexander. It was a feeder class to the larger Prison Creative Arts Project at the university. Judith Tannenbaum's memoir, *Disguised as a Poem,* was required reading. She wrote about the power of art and poetry and human connection that could take shape behind the barren cement walls of prison. Her book left a deep impression on me. It gave me the courage to reach out to her personally when a crisis in the class left me feeling betrayed by the very social justice community I identified so closely with.

As part of the syllabus for English 319, students had paired up and gone into carceral settings—prisons, juvenile halls—to collaborate on original plays with the men, women, and youth inside. In the classroom, we learned about the prison-industrial complex, the "school-to-prison" pipeline, and the various social injustices and inequities embedded in our world. We dissected different approaches to fighting inequality and where and how art, writing, theater, and creative expression could be used as tools in the fight.

We seemed to be all in it together, but one day the unity of the class was shattered. Lines were drawn about whether you could be a true activist and "in it for the long haul" if you weren't motivated by rage. A yelling match ensued between those on the side of rage and the rest of us.

There were tears and red faces. Angry students left the room, slamming the door behind them. I stayed behind, frozen in my seat, my inner experiences attacked with a level of vitriol and disdain that I had assumed were reserved only for perpetrators of social injustice. I hadn't known there was a "right" way to feel. After all, weren't we all in this together? What did it matter what emotional underpinnings brought each of us to the work, so long as we showed up with respect, curiosity, and integrity?

Judith had written so beautifully about love and connection in her book, and I had felt so motivated by that same hope. Of course, I was angered by so many of the world's injustices, but it was the possibility for human connection and hope and growth that motivated me. Yet here we were in this class, tearing one another down and pointing fingers about who was "truly committed."

I felt completely abandoned by the professor and my classmates. In retrospect, this was my first exposure to a now all too familiar scenario of divisiveness among those on the political Left. That night, I found Judith's email address online and sent her a message in desperation. I asked her where love and hope fit into the narrative of the "long haul" work for social change. She wrote back that same evening, inviting a dialogue in which she asked more questions than she gave answers.

Her response became the first of many long email exchanges and encounters that shaped my thinking about corrections and accompanied me into adulthood. The spring after graduation, I moved from Michigan to the Bay Area in California for a job at a law firm that focused on prisoners' rights. Over brunch at Judith's home, where she served home-baked applesauce cake, our friendship took seed. Over fifteen years, Judith became a friend and mentor, a kind of "California Jewish" mother (familiar in many ways as my own Brooklyn-born Jewish mother, but with her own unique way of flowing in the world, which I can only describe as "California"). She watched me move through various social justice jobs, go through the ups and downs of breakups, new relationships, and graduate school. She was the first guest to arrive at my wedding and visited me soon after I gave birth to my first son. She usually brought applesauce cake with her. In many ways, I "grew up" around Judith.

I was born and raised in the Midwest, and much of my mental map of the Bay Area is marked by the various cultural events I attended with Judith. Even more crucially, her invitations expanded my appreciation for the connections between art and justice. There were readings in independent bookstores scattered throughout the Bay; political plays in basement theaters in the Mission District and community theaters in Berkeley; a production of *Hamlet* performed in and around Alcatraz; a choral piece sung at a church in the Outer Richmond neighborhood, with Spoon Jackson's poems as the lyrics; talks and social justice–related films at UC Berkeley, Stanford, local libraries, and community spaces; and art exhibits in San Francisco.

After most events, particularly the political ones, we sent a flurry of emails back and forth. Judith always wanted to reflect and ask questions, and pushed me to do the same. Whose voices were allowed in the room? Whose weren't? How did whatever speaker or conference or panel discussion fit into larger conversations about prisons, or art, or social change?

Often, she wanted feedback on an op-ed she was writing, usually related to prison reform. We connected, too, over our personal social anxieties—our discomfort in large groups, the need for validation after either of us spoke up or spoke out at a conference or a public forum (Did I sound too critical? Did I even make sense?).

When Judith spoke publicly, while always respectful and with a stance of openness to dialogue, there could also be an urgency and underlying fierceness in her tone—a need to protect the ideas and voices of people inside of prison from misrepresentation or exploitation. I felt honored and privileged to watch Judith model strength in voicing her opinions, while also experiencing the same self-criticism and insecurities that I had thought were unique to me as a young person.

Judith's living room was a place to ask and discuss big questions about policy, movements, and organizing. The architecture was unremarkable: a ranch-style one-bedroom house built in the 1970s—small single-pane windows, flat white walls, low ceilings, an old brown shag carpet, wood paneling, and brown-and-yellow linoleum in the kitchen. Yet Judith created depth and light and color in that space.

From the hallway ceiling, she hung a string of colorful tissue paper doilies. They moved in the slightest breeze and created a play of light and shadow on the walls. A philodendron vine climbed the wall and encircled the perimeter of the ceiling of her living room like a living crown. On the walls, she hung images of hands (holding one another, reaching out, painted with Indigenous designs). I never asked what drew her to the imagery, a recurring motif in her art, but I like to think they represented humanness, connection, and story.

For many years, Judith invited me and two other University of Michigan graduates (and former members of the Prison Creative Arts Project) for a potluck meal each month. Judith always baked. We formed a special little group—a friendship based on a shared experience of having worked inside prisons.

This room was an incubator of sorts. We discussed what we were hearing from the people we knew inside prison. And we also held space to ask deeply personal questions about events in our young adult lives. At times, her living room also became a salon of sorts, where she invited various guests to discuss their prison arts work.

She was a connector, and I would leave invigorated, energized, ready to tackle whatever big question I was dealing with at the time, whether it was personal or social justice–related. She had an ability to be fully present and to listen deeply. She was interested in seeking realness in others, humanness, in finding connection, pushing ideas and dialogue forward, and in shining a light on the depths of our truths and stories.

During the last four years of our friendship, I moved from the East Bay to the South Bay and we saw each other less and less. We emailed every so often with updates and I sent her photos of my son. After my mother died, Judith wanted so badly to visit and hold my second-born son but was in too much pain to travel. Instead, we spoke on the phone of life and death and peace and gratitude. Judith died a month later.

In the end, Judith answered my question of what it means to do long-haul social justice work, but not in words. She revealed the answer by living it and inviting me to participate. She taught me that the work is about finding the humanness in others. It is seeking opportunities for connection and engagement with one another again and again. It is showing up, despite fear. It is supporting and nurturing one another. It is breaking applesauce cake in the living room with an open door. It is creating and finding color and depth and shape where there seemingly are none.

Seeing Beyond: A Love Letter

Barbara Schaefer

Dear Judith,

After my project *Love Letter to Roma*, I have been contemplating my next step. What worked for me in the project, and the overall feedback I received, was that it came from a sincere, heartfelt place, which is my love for Roma. To deepen my expression of love, not only for Roma, my idea is that I will write individual letters (love letters) to people I love and am grateful for. Then, in some way—I'm not sure exactly how yet—I will combine the letters with visual and sound elements.

With the sudden news of the end of your life, which may not have been sudden but is to me, I am beginning this project by writing to you. Regardless of the project, I would have written you this letter. You are the most eloquent writer I know and sharing words with you seems appropriate.

Beginning in Taos with the ease of walking or biking between our respective studios, I felt joy and solidarity in sharing time: inspiring talks, walks on the Morada, and the solace of partaking in the life of art making. I remember wishes we whispered to stones as we placed them on the crosses at the Morada. Although the stones may have become displaced, I sense that somehow they are still there, and deep within, the wishes are spread in the universe, invisible but potent, like indestructible energy. Somehow our steps have formed a path that has kept us in each other's lives, sometimes more and sometimes less, but present.

I remember how you came to help me in Taos during a bout of vertigo, how you later described my movements as rocking and keening to keep the malign entity at bay. Or were you the one moving as a shaman moves to help the possessed rid the body of an illness? I felt your presence as a light filtering into the room. Although I didn't see, wasn't able to see, that light then, somehow I see it now. And I see it because you brought it into the room and into my consciousness, and it shines through the years. I always said that you are perfect except for your speed, but in that moment you were slow, calm, and light itself; someone I felt safe with and wanted close, a place I was drawn to from afar. I knew I would eventually see there was light amid all that pain.

Perhaps while you are lying on the floor in that almost comfortable position, you are beckoning the light. Perhaps all that light—light behind, in front of, and in between layers of light—is what you saw and felt during all the looking and seeing you wrote about in that amazing book, "Looking at Looking." Perhaps the light is transforming you day by day as you unload what is no longer needed and transition from pain to another form or formlessness. As you move into lightness, my guess and wish are that there will no longer be pain, even before the end.

I remember your telling me that when the numbers all show up the same on the digital clock, you identify with the 11:11. Toward the end, you told me you weighed 111 pounds and it struck me there is some correlation, though I don't know what. I always think of you when I see all ones.

Throughout the years that I have known you, you have taught me about words. When we met in Taos, I had recently returned to the United States, and after twelve years in Roma, my words were a blur. Not only because of the difference in language but also because I had to grow into them. You recognized potential in some of my early poems, and in spending time with you, your honesty and truth in your own speak, I learned more about words. It wasn't only the written word but also the spoken one. I was always in awe of your speaking and the quality of your deep and rich voice.

I remember a walk we took around a lake in the Bay Area some years ago and how our communication lifted me into a higher and deeper realm. Those conversations are still there, echoing and sparkling like the stones at the Morada, indecipherable but radiant. I know I wasn't and am still not an easy or good student and initially react badly to most criticism, no matter how constructive. Nonetheless, I have learned to keep asking more of myself, thanks to you. I have come to understand the importance and the danger of words.

I was honored and happy when you came to New York and chose to stay with me, even when you were coming for other reasons. You said that you felt best with me and at my place. I hope that I, too, have given you something significant over the years. I saw you grow visually, or, as I said of myself, and I believe you said of me regarding writing, you grew into an understanding and heightened use of the visual. I believe this filling out and understanding other forms of art are enriching and part of the evolution of an artist, though not a given. For example, the book you wrote on looking and seeing showed evidence of this sensitivity. To me, it speaks of your whole person; beauty, truth, kindness, and wisdom inherent in all the various aspects of you and your evolution as artist and woman.

I hope that in whatever ways I have disappointed or not been there for you in the way you wanted, you have forgiven. As in most relationships, there have been bumps in the road, but even from a physical distance, we have always found a way back to the care and love between us. Your generosity, thoughtfulness, and kindness are remarkable, and have made me aware that I can always do better.

When we first met in Taos, I told you about my very first friend, Judy, and how I had the sense that meeting you was symbolic and telling. I was thrilled to have another Judy in my life. And even better, a Judith!

Thank you for all the innumerable times you helped me: with words, with clarifying ideas, with poems, for caring about me, for holiday poems that now adorn my refrigerator, along with a poem for the journey, for so many things you shared, for seeing me, for seeing beyond me, for your love and, always, good wishes, for being entirely who you are, for your warmth, generosity, intelligence, and kind heart.

With gratitude and love,
  Barbara

Breathing

Tenesha Smith

Dear Judith,
So far so good.

There is so much to say to you that I don't know where to begin. I just wanna talk to you. Or just walk with you and think out loud.

Tenesha

★ ★ ★

I looked forward to the envelopes with her distinctive writing. I always found a quiet space to read her letters. I always wanted to know what she thought of the last thing I had written to her. I always wanted to know about where her artistry was leading her.

Me, I've always been trapped in the space between not so much of anything and all of everything. I was seventeen years old when we met. I was going to an alternative high school. I liked most of my classmates. They were middle-class white teens; Goth, with black hair and lipstick; hip-hop fans with baggy jeans and T-shirts; punk rock and pierced, and everything in between. They tried so hard to be different that they were all just alike, the offspring of hippies and liberals. Also attending were Black and Mexican kids who were transplants from Richmond and Oakland, looking for a calm place to regroup after whatever trauma they had experienced. I was one of the latter. We were our own Breakfast Club.

Judith was an artist in residence, and when she first walked into the classroom she brought what I thought was a nervous energy; brown hair that looked like she'd just gotten out of the shower and hadn't dried it; Birkenstocks, a long flowery skirt, and a long-sleeved teal top. She moved her hands around a lot when she spoke, quick, short movements. She was always asking a lot of questions. My first thought when meeting her was, Why are white people like this?

★ ★ ★

Hi Tenesha

I was thinking about getting you to the UK. I know you did not ask for my opinion, but here are some thoughts I had about ways to make this happen . . .

Judith

★ ★ ★

At that time in my life, I didn't really know how to carry a dream yet. I didn't know how to plant it and nurture it until fruition. I understood the push part of life, the labor. I knew how to survive. I knew how to accept. I knew how to write poetry, tuck it into the spine of a book, and pretend it wasn't there.

I didn't really exist. The words I put on paper did not exist. I had literally slept for two years after being overwhelmed by depression. I was trying to remember how to breathe on purpose.

Judith would later tell the story of how brave I was to volunteer to be the first one to read my poem at an open mic in San Francisco. Judith had invited students from her writing class to meet up with her to attend an open-mike event in the Haight district on a Saturday afternoon.

I studied the dirty sidewalk as we walked to the youth center that operated as a safe house for homeless children.

I walked to the podium, my poem clutched in my hand— a crinkled-up piece of paper that I had stuffed into my pocket. I knew all about movement and the migration of a physical body. I knew how to go through the motions, always looking for an easier way to do life. My seventeen-year-old self was tired already. I went to the podium because I had decided to inhale blank pieces of paper and exhale through my pen, through my pencils. Judith did not know it at the time, but I used her as a raft. I floated on what I viewed as her idealism. But, really, one foot in front of the other was very practical.

I am still figuring out what story I'm trying to tell. I just know I used to be dead. I had to remember how to be alive. I needed someone to carry my dreams for me until I learned to carry them for myself.

* * *

Dear Judith,

A long time ago, you gave me a postcard that featured windows and doorways. It was set in either Harlem or some other very urban setting from the fifties. I took that postcard wherever I went for years, tucked into whatever journal or book I was reading. I was inspired by the imagery of doors and windows. From that inspiration came many poems, many I still have.

Before you transition, I want you to know that I was inspired by all of our conversations. You got to give the last gift.

Tenesha

A Place Called Human

Spoon Jackson

Judith sent me a postcard a week before she died. It was a prayer by Saint Francis, Judith wrote. "This is a prayer I used to say walking into Quentin. Even though I'm Jewish. End getting closer."

I have discovered from my studies during my incarceration that one must be authentic and real like a newborn for any change or learning to take place. I learned to hold on like a badger to what is true and let go of what is fake. I feel Judith as surely as I feel the wind on my face and see the stars in the sky.

* * *

It felt awkward when I first started going to groups at San Quentin. Everything was new to me. San Quentin was big-city living compared to the small desert town I came from. I felt shy and was silent but had my eyes, ears, heart, mind, and spirit wide open like a desert sky. I sat in self-help groups and discovered many cats had their group or chrono face on. A facade just to get credit for a group. The more real each person in a group is, the deeper and richer the group becomes. It's like slow-brewing tea.

I had played sports with some of those same dudes on the yard. I could see they thought of the groups as playthings. Yes, game playing and group face can happen anywhere in the world—schools, churches, social and political institutions, and other functions.

I decided to be my true self and at that time I walked in silence. I was silent everywhere, even in groups. I soaked in what I could and gave out one-word answers and looks, or nodded my head yes or no. My mantra of life became "Speak when I can improve on silence." I believed it would be best to listen to allow the knowledge and wisdom in any group to settle inside me—to seep into my heart and spirit.

The first time I went to Judith's poetry class in the dungeon classroom, I saw many of the same guys I had played sports with. But I was stunned these same guys did not have their group or chrono faces on. Their realness, love, wisdom, and authenticity shined out like globes or magical orbs. Judith had mastered how to bring out the real through the art of poetry.

Judith would model for the drawing and painting class. She would bring in guests—guest artists and educators. She strived to find or create a medium where prisoners and staff could meet safely, honestly, and creatively in the middle of a place called human.

Finally, after a year of silence and one individual consultation in the dungeon classroom with Judith, we knew we had a kinship and a natural connection that could never end, even after her death.

Every morning after our individual meeting, I rushed out of my cell in West Block at San Quentin to meet with Judith at the Arts in Corrections (AIC) office. Jim Carlson would be at his desk. Jim had the foresight to hire Judith as poetry instructor for AIC. Usually when I came to the office, I had a new poem or poem revision. Sometimes one of us had a burning question we needed to share and discuss.

Monday mornings were special. I sat on the stoop in front of the Education Building and waited for Judith to come into the plaza through huge black metal castlelike doors. I almost walked in her footsteps to the AIC office. I arrived just in time to get Judith's homemade chocolate chip cookies. She shared them freely with staff and prisoners. Everyone had their coffee or milk and waited like baby sparrows to be fed.

We were inspired to be ourselves in Judith's classes. We met one another where we all needed to meet on a human landscape and feelings were okay. We shared our hearts, voices, visions, and journeys, in our own ways.

Judith helped process and bring in hundreds of guests for the Samuel Beckett play *Waiting for Godot.* She had no problem speaking to staff or prisoners when she felt slighted. When she saw, felt, or vibed something unique—your voice or a niche— she helped cultivate that vision and then she would get out of the way.

Whenever Judith said she would do something it was as good as done. I cannot recall one writing or art project or task together that was not accomplished. I came up with the idea for our memoir. Judith came up with the title *By Heart* and the idea of alternating chapters. *By Heart* for the heart of our journeys together, sharing realness and a love of wisdom, truth, and the arts.

Except we never got the chance to share a stage in the free world. We wanted to travel, do poetry, and speak to people in real time. We tried everything we could to make that happen by my being released from prison physically. In the end, the walls were much higher and steeper to navigate than we had hoped.

* * *

Even if you were like me, silent in her class, Judith embraced that silence. My silence did not intimidate her. She shared a similar silence. She found wisdom in the silence. Judith shared that appreciation of the silence with guest artists. She had ways to dive into the silence and have it glow. I think that is why the forest and the trees were especially sacred to her. Judith could hear them even in her silence.

* * *

Fire

Judith was like a fire
on a chilly morning
where we gathered around
and gained warmth
and insight

She ignited our fire
(at our core)
that often we did
not know we had

Fire she then gathered
around and gained
warmth and insight

Judith knew there was
something special
undiscovered
about each of us

Especially those of us
she allowed to be
closer to her

We all grew
like a stand of sequoias
sharing space

★ ★ ★

How Judith knew about her upcoming death months ahead
of time, then weeks and days, I don't know; that is beyond my
ken. But at times it seemed like she made a reservation to trans-
form—to die. As if she knew when and where she was going.
A poet's retreat beyond the sky. I am sure Judith was prepared

for whatever would come. She rested easy like smooth blues, jazz, or folk songs. She made it clear everyone was welcome at the fire. Starlight does not wane—it transforms.

Broken to Whole

Boston Woodard

I first met Judith while I was serving my sentence in San Quentin
State Prison in 1985. She had only been there a couple of months
when we met. Her supervisor was San Quentin's arts facilitator,
Jim Carlson, who oversaw all the Arts in Corrections (AIC)
groups and programs that were becoming available for several
years under his leadership. Jim arranged programs not only for
the prisoners on San Quentin's Main Line but for those in Ad-
ministrative Segregation (the Hole), as well.

I was involved with the AIC through the music program
in what is now called "the old Education Building." That was
where artists and teachers like Judith would gather with Jim to
discuss art program matters. I remember Judith sorting papers,
organizing supplies for her class, and making sure she made
extra copies of her students' poems so they could send them
home to their families. She was a stickler for details regarding
her agenda.

Judith's poetry class was in one of several rooms downstairs.
At the end of the hall were the institution's TV control room
and two band rooms full of music equipment. I spent most of
my spare time practicing the bass guitar or learning new songs
with my band. My friend Spoon Jackson was in Judith's class
and would encourage me to "check it out." He knew I was also
getting into writing, but it was strictly nonfiction. I told Spoon
I couldn't write a poem if my life depended on it. I asked Judith
if I could sit in on her class if I stayed out of the way. She said
I could come when I wasn't in the band room. I was grateful
for that.

I remember once Spoon opened the door to the band room and told me Judith was upstairs with cookies and that I'd better hurry up. She would bring homemade cookies every week for staff and her students. By the time I got to the AIC office, sure enough, all the cookies were gone. But on my way back downstairs, Judith handed me a napkin with several cookies wrapped inside. That was Judith. The cookie thing may seem trivial, but to a prisoner who rarely had something homemade, Judith's cookies were a big deal.

Despite my misgivings, I did write some poems in Judith's class. She would also allow me to write one-hundred- to three-hundred-word pieces from prompts, which she critiqued for me. Many times she said, "Use your imagination, Boston; picture what you want to say in your head." I do that to this day.

Through her class, I also overcame my biggest fear: public speaking. Every week she would have the guys read what they wrote from a small wooden podium in front of the class. It's because of Judith and the encouragement of her students in San Quentin that I'm able to speak publicly today.

In 1986, I got a job as a clerk on San Quentin's Death Row when it was located in C-Section. In 1988, Death Row was moved to East Block, where it is today. At that time, I was one of two prisoners from the Main Line allowed to go onto "the Row." We got the job because we had no drugs on our records and were never part of a gang. During that time, Judith began working with men on the Row and in the Hole.

Lynnelle, another amazing AIC teacher, had been working with the condemned men for some time. She taught Judith the ropes on how to teach in such a high-security part of the prison. When either of them came to the Row, the door officer, "Chili," would key them in, and allow me or the other clerk to help them with the boxes of approved art supplies. We were allowed to carry the supplies to the top of the stairs but no farther.

Judith almost always had a smile on her face. Even now when I reflect back on those days, it's her smile I remember. When Judith was in teaching mode, she was all business. But her smile was infectious, putting everyone in a better mood. To many of the men, Judith was like a big sister. She treated everyone with equal respect.

In 1989, San Quentin State Prison was transforming into a lower-level institution. Spoon and I, and hundreds of others, were herded into buses and moved to the newly opened New Folsom State Prison. Judith was losing many students who had been with her for three to four years—students with whom she had come to develop a mutual respect and thoroughly enjoyed teaching. I know she left not too long after that.

I began writing articles and stories for various outside (free world) publications about what was going on behind prison walls. My book, *Inside the Broken California Prison System,* was published in 2011. The next year, Judith set up a reading from my book and those of three other prison authors—Spoon Jackson, Ken Hartman, and Jarvis Masters—at Litquake, which is San Francisco's annual literary festival. Our friends and relatives read for us in what was the first time Litquake had ever included prisoner writings in the reading program. I will forever be grateful to Judith for that opportunity.

Twenty-four years after being in other prisons, I was transferred back to San Quentin as a low-custody-level prisoner when I had three to four years left on my sentence. Judith visited me several times during those final years. It was a short drive across the Richmond–San Rafael Bridge to San Quentin from her home, which made it easy for her.

During one of the last in-person conversations we had, I remember telling her I was nervous about finally getting out after so many years. She told me, "You got this, Boston, I promise you." My life became much better with people like Judith

Tannenbaum in it. She inspired me by example. I will never forget her.

I've been out going on four years now. I'm off parole and feeling good about my life. I work, and live in a nice home with a car and great friends. I am involved in community events and activities, and have become that contributing member to society Judith told me I would be.

You were right, Judith: I got this.

Imaginary Landscapes

Fury Young

I was lucky enough to know Judith for the last five years of her life, and during that time, the formative half decade of my mid- to late twenties, I came to view her as a mentor and kindred spirit.

As a teacher, Judith possessed consistency, honesty, and humility. When you read her memoir, *Disguised as a Poem,* which she once told me was her best work, you will find someone who sought hard truths in dark places. From those dark places, she made lifelong friends.

When it came to her poetry, Judith's words were the geology of California and far beyond. She read with a steady and soft voice that birds might envy.

As a colleague, Judith was, again, consistent. There wasn't an email she didn't reply to or a question she didn't answer— sometimes in unexpected intricate detail!

Though I only got to meet Judith twice in person, those two visits were special to me, like visiting a spiritual adviser whom long travel had brought you to.

The old saying "You can't take it with you" has never made sense to me. Though Judith is no longer here, I'll take her with me when I'm in a prison, workshopping songs with incarcerated musicians, or when I write a poem that I seek to be open but harsh like she was.

When I left Judith the second and last time I saw her, she was lying down on a rug in her apartment in El Cerrito, head toward the ceiling, looking at an imaginary landscape. She'd told me that most of her recent days had been spent in this position, with a New Orleans radio station keeping her company as nostalgic sound track.

Upon leaving her apartment, I knew I would never see her again. A part of me wanted to give her a big hug or make a heartfelt statement, but the fact that I'd traveled across the country to see her said enough. So I settled for a no-frills "Have a good rest of your day," and I opened the door to leave. With a hand circling over her head like a halo, Judith replied, "Thank you so much. It's all gonna be up here."

In that moment, Judith gave me another thing to take with me. An eternal sense of wonder that lay right between the ears, that transcended death and soared over canyons. That perched on redwoods and then kept on soaring, that still lands on my shoulder every once in a poetic while.

Running with Judith

Luis J. Rodriguez

Judith Tannenbaum and I first met at a national conference of prison writing facilitators in the mid-nineties. She was teaching poetry at California's San Quentin State Prison, something she'd done for years throughout the state's myriad prison and juvenile facilities. I was doing poetry readings, talks, and writing workshops at state prisons, juvenile lockups, and jails in Illinois, where I lived at the time.

There were only a few of us writers then entering locked facilities to awaken the poet/scribe among incarcerated men, women, and youth. At the conference, there were maybe a hundred or so from around the country.

Judith told me she'd been using my memoir, *Always Running, La Vida Loca, Gang Days in L.A.*, in her classes. The book, released in 1993, became one of two at the time about Los Angeles' gangs that sparked global interest after the 1992 L.A. uprising following the acquittal of police officers in the beating of Rodney King. I knew about the subject—having been a barrio gang youth since age eleven, in and out of jails and juvenile hall, and a drug addict for seven years. I left *la vida loca* ("the crazy life") at twenty, around the time I married, obtained a job at a local steel mill, and held my first child in my arms. I also became active in social justice issues against poverty and police abuse, and in advocating writing and the arts as healing and liberating acts.

Even though I lived in Chicago for fifteen years, Los Angeles was my home. I have been working in prisons in some capacity since 1980, when I helped facilitate a writing class at California's Chino State Prison. I was twenty-six. My mentor at the time was Manual "Manazar" Gamboa, who became clean and sober and crime-free after doing seventeen years in prisons and shooting up heroin for twenty. Manazar helped guide a group of young writers from the greater East Los Angeles area through the L.A. Latino Writers Association (LALWA). I was one of them.

While I labored in industry and construction, I still wrote. I carried a bag of scribbling with me to LALWA workshops, where I found an embracing community. Over the years, my readings, talks, and teaching circles in prisons also took me throughout California—San Quentin, Soledad, Folsom, California Institute for Women, and Lancaster prisons, as well as juvenile halls, probation camps, jails, and parolee housing. I did the same in eighteen states. And because of my reputation, I've visited prisons or worked with incarcerated youth in Mexico, El Salvador, Guatemala, Nicaragua, Argentina, Italy, and England.

In Judith, I found a kindred spirit. After our initial meeting, we stayed in touch by mail. We shared ideas, bad and good experiences, as well as becoming touchstones for each other in this work. She introduced me to Spoon Jackson, who, she said, was an extraordinary writer. Spoon and I also corresponded by mail. Over the years, I've corresponded with hundreds of incarcerated persons and teachers in incarcerated settings. I particularly appreciated these letters from Judith and Spoon.

In the year 2000, I returned to California, where in a year's time I helped create Tia Chucha's Centro Cultural & Bookstore in the northeast San Fernando Valley. We're situated in a mostly Mexican/Central American community of half a million people that had no bookstores, movie houses, art galleries, or comprehensive cultural spaces until we opened our doors. We now serve twenty thousand people in all the arts, also hosting art exhibits, open-mic events, a literacy and arts festival, and much more. Judith came by to read from the book she wrote with Spoon: *By Heart: Poetry, Prison, and Two Lives.*

I also continued working behind bars.

In 2007, I began a yearlong creative writing class in the state prison in Lancaster (California State Prison–Los Angeles County). I took a break for a few years, until I returned to the same facility in 2016 for the Alliance for California Traditional Arts. I'd been doing between thirteen and fifteen creative writing sessions in two high-security yards since then, until the 2020 pandemic halted all in-person instruction.

One day in 2016 on A yard, I saw the name Stanley Jackson on the list of students who had signed up for my class. It took me a while, but I began to recall this was Spoon's birth name. I had never met Spoon, so I wouldn't have recognized him. I looked around and asked who Stanley Jackson was. An older gentleman in braids raised his hand. What a pleasure it was to finally meet Spoon! As I knew he would, he contributed powerful pieces and even recited Shakespeare from memory. Spoon's work appeared in the 2020 anthology I did of writings from my class, entitled *Make a Poem Cry,* edited by Kenneth E. Hartman and myself (Tia Chucha Press).

When I learned Judith had passed at the end of 2019, my heart broke. Judith left an enduring legacy of writing and arts for the most marginalized. In the process, she helped a whole society reimagine a world without prisons, without punishment, instead integrated with healing and transformative arts as a powerful path to redemption. I wish I had spoken to her more. That we'd written each other more. But as prisoners know, regrets only line the cracked walls of a broken house. I continue this work—now that there are thousands doing similar work throughout the United States. I will do this in the spirit and memory of an amazing woman, poet, and teacher, Judith Tannenbaum.

In the verse of the dreaming eye,
no walls, no bars, can hinder the flow
of words, images, sounds, tastes.
Such is poetry, and such is what teachers who draw
  out poetry must do.

Judith was my friend, my comrade in arms,
only these arms are metaphor, sense, and beauty.
I am in her revolution, a rhyme warrior,
who also teaches the forgotten,
that they are re-membered,
that their voices amidst the silence
  are thunder and nectar;
  the sweet in the scars,
  the roar in the rumination.

Twenty-five Years of Walking with Judith

Janet Heller

For nearly half of my life, I took walks with Judith Tannenbaum. Up and down Solano Avenue, circling Mount Tamalpais, and around Lake Merritt we walked and talked and listened. I met Judith in the summer of 1994. At the age of forty-seven, she was a writer and a well-known community artist or teaching artist who had taught poetry in the schools and in the prisons. As a twenty-nine-year-old queer teacher, poet, and community artist from Florida, I could not have been more different. But we walked and talked together for twenty-five years—I always on her right because she had mobility issues with her neck. By her side, I always felt like I could arrive at any destination and explore any problem with her.

In 1994, I had moved to San Francisco to start a Peace Corps–like program for writers called San Francisco WritersCorps. A national initiative that came from a marriage between AmeriCorps and the National Endowment for the Arts, it was inspired by the Works Progress Administration, which created jobs for artists. Judith's name was on a short list of Bay Area distinguished writers and teachers, and I was told to call her. I was so grateful that she made time for me and was generous with her advice.

Her deep voice on the phone did not match her small frame, but her mind was like the MacArthur Maze, a web of interstate highways, bridges, conduits, railroad tracks, and heaps of deserted roadside orange poppies near the San Francisco–Oakland Bay Bridge. She was a walking think tank, and I loved being in her company, whether we talked books, family, movies, politics, travel, or writing. It was usually all of the above. She was a true friend, but from 1997 to 2010, I was also her boss at WritersCorps, which she liked to say when she introduced me to someone. "This is Janet. She was the best boss."

My first walk with Judith was during my first visit to Berkeley, California, where Judith was teaching poetry, writing, and deeply engaged in social justice work inside prisons. She was the perfect greeter for the Bay Area's progressive and complex arts scene. Judith prized time and was one of the most efficient workers and thinkers I ever met. She observed everything. She watched with the most exquisite care. She had a wicked sense of humor and was a serious intellectual all at the same time. She could be open-minded and deeply opinionated. She tolerated no bullshit.

It was fun to make Judith laugh, because her smile shot directly back at you through magically squinty eyes. We had a love of humor, quick wit steeped in a shared Jewish heritage. For twenty-five years, Judith was one of my closest friends. Her care and caution, pessimism, and hesitancy were a perfect match for my optimistic, jump-in spirit. She was an ally and a friend and I trusted her completely to speak her mind, which could be rich, dark, blue, lyrical, reflecting light and shadow.

So each walk would begin with "You stand here" or "Can you get on my right side?" and then we were off. Walks around town in her sweet neighborhood in El Cerrito could be to the post office, as Judith was an avid writer and sender of cards, notes, gifts, and maintained many, many friendships. She never forgot my birthday or the birthdays of my kids. It gave her joy to connect and "send LOVE," which is the way she ended most emails and letters.

* * *

In April 2005, in Vancouver's Stanley Park, we walked for six hours, buoyed by the light reflecting off the Burrard Inlet, English Bay, and Coal Harbour, talking, dreaming, and scheming.

I had recently lost a late pregnancy and was tender from the disappointment. The water, the light, the deep green of the trees, and the air gave me new energy and strength. Walking with Judith always gave me pleasure. During that particular walk, we dreamed up an anthology of children's poetry she would edit, inspired by the anniversary of the 1906 earthquake.

"Hi, Janet!" Judith always greeted me from her small El Cerrito apartment, which was her home/office, surrounded by books and by posters of the dancer Judith Jamison and a *Waiting for Godot* performance by her San Quentin students. She suffered from debilitating pain from neck, back, shoulders, and feet. Walking was something she could do and loved doing. Seeing trees, water, and sky, her mind would leave her aching body and soar, and she would take me with her. Judith taught me about the importance of the artist in the world, and we developed a beautiful program together that placed over one hundred writers in schools, libraries, and detention centers. She cared deeply about sharing the work she loved with the next generation and worked for decades to share best practices and provide love and encouragement. She was the WritersCorps' training coordinator by title, but she was a devoted mentor.

For eight years, our small group of teaching artists gathered each February at Green Gulch Farm Zen Center, near Muir Beach, to rest, walk, play, and plan together, and take a breath before the final four months of the school year, which involved teaching, editing, publishing, and celebrating the writing of young people in San Francisco. At night in the Lindisfarne Guest House, we gathered around the woodstove and played games. Somebody always brought an instrument. It was heaven for me and I cherished these times away from home to work more deeply with a beautiful team of writers—mostly Black, brown, and queer. During one game, Judith was flat on her back, resting quietly on a green futon cushion while we played Dictionary.

Someone picked a word that appeared in Yiddish stories. No one in the group had heard of it. Judith rose up like a ghost from a Polish shetl and said in a stern voice, "Don't you remember your Isaac Bashevis Singer!" and promptly lay back down and went still.

As our work lives separated and I took a break to write and teach, we remained friends sometimes distanced, but my deep love and respect never waned. As I began to form the program I run now, Chapter 510 & the Dept. of Make Believe, Oakland's youth writing center, our walks near San Francisco Bay would end. She always sent me home with books, art supplies, advice, and later furniture, which would become the first pieces we used to assemble our writing sanctuary in downtown Oakland.

When I look at these pieces—a curvy wooden love seat, chairs from her parents' living room, a writer's desk with a drop-down top she bought in 1964, the year I was born—I feel Judith nearby. When she struggled to travel after breaking her wrist, I would send her photographs of teenagers scribbling over composition notebooks, writing and rocking away in her mother's yellow upholstered chair or her father's brown leather recliner. I was so lucky to be a recipient of Judith's attention, generosity, warmth, and devotion. I grieved, knowing our walks would end as her health deteriorated, but I am realizing now that they have taken a new form. Because Judith is free, she can be on either side of me as I walk and listen, her voice light and laughing in the bright light.

Talk to Judith

Leah Joki

When I became the institutional artist facilitator at Chuckawalla Valley State Prison in Blythe, California, I sat in an empty space with only a desk, chair, and a word processor. The director of Arts in Corrections, Jim Carlson, advised me to talk with Judith Tannenbaum. When I reached out to Susan Hill, the director of Artreach at UCLA, she recommended that I talk to Judith Tannenbaum. When I spoke with my facilitator colleagues Tom Skelly, Jack Bowers, and Kim Kaufman, they all said, "You should talk to Judith Tannenbaum."

So I did. I talked to Judith Tannenbaum. The advice I got from Judith, which has stuck with me for my entire career over the last three decades, was this: "Always enjoy the time you have in the classroom, inside prison." And "Stay calm. Don't sweat the small stuff."

It seems like simple advice, but it was profound: It is imperative for teaching artists in prison to enjoy their time inside. If you don't enjoy being there, it probably isn't the right place for you. It is also important to understand that being there, in the classroom with inmate participants, is a privilege. As we know, many mountains were moved to pave the path for us to sit there in that stark classroom. Never, ever take that for granted. Because, as we also know, that privilege can be taken away.

And, of course, staying calm was how Judith lived her whole life. In her calmness is where you saw those captivating eyes just cheering you on to write, write, and then write some more. And in her calmness, her engaging, joyful smile emerged and everything always just felt better somehow.

Judith's diligence and commitment to her craft was an inspiration to many of us. When Arts in Corrections was still a toddler of a program, she was the mother ship that many of us followed. She encouraged us to work calmly, with joy, and then to produce work that wasn't just good work but great. She set the bar high, and by golly we jumped as high as we could. And then she smiled that joyous smile with the captivating eyes.

"You Must Feel the Rocks Beneath Your Feet"

devorah major

December 2020—A Year After

Dear Judith,

I am thinking about you. Thinking about qualities of friendships that touch and change our lives. We knew each other over decades, our daughters turning from toddlers to young women, our books sliding out with all of the pains and urgencies of birthing our young, each of us traveling the country and working our craft. Yet in those years, we talked face-to-face only one or two dozen times. It seems right to say that we were tea poets. We drank tea and talked poems and poets, teaching and children, plans and dreams and quiet desires, and sustained struggles. I remember sitting with you at your kitchen table, both of us laughing long over some story or another. And at my kitchen table, looking at how the years had twisted and turned. There was a table in a crepes café, sitting on a high school bench after or before a guest teaching spot, on the phone sometimes, and tea was usually a part of it.

I remember how you were packing up your home and preparing to go from writing retreat to writing retreat for the next year or so and my quiet sighs, for I wanted to have both that courage and freedom. My son was nearly grown and my daughter able, but I still couldn't see the space. But within a year, I found myself at a retreat in Connecticut, watching blue herons alight near the pond on the summer evenings. Your journey was something you not only wanted but needed to do. It helped fuel me to at least take a bite of that sweet apple.

When I think of you, it is your wide-open smile that I most remember, warm and welcoming, and making others sparkle, lighting up your students, friends, and, I am sure, your family. We both liked to laugh and knew what it was to cry. We both found our ways into and through our poet-teacher lives, learning at least as much as we taught. That is something I so value about you. You were a river learning each curve of the riverbank, learning each fish that swam your waters, each river reed reaching up toward the sun. You were always looking, asking, and seeing with a humility and kindness that you wished for the world.

I looked forward each December to your year-end wisdom. Some line or thought that inspired. I am moving and my books and papers are packed and the last thin slip of paper you sent lay carefully in one of the boxes. It said that to cross the river you must feel the rocks beneath your feet. The waters surge, but my feet are steady on the smooth, flattened rocks. Thank you.

Judith, you created the world you wanted to live in. The people who came to honor you had ancestors from all over the globe, spoke more than one language. There were four generations, from toddlers through seasoned elders, artists of life, if not practitioners of a formal art. It was a statement of your love for the planet, love for humanity, and love for poetry and music. It was all you, Judith. Your presence as poet, as woman, as mother, as friend, and now as poet spirit has touched and changed me and I am grateful.

With enduring respect and love,
devorah

My Odyssey with Judith

Neelanjana Bannerjee

The etymology of the word *mentor* comes from Homer's epic *The Odyssey*. Odysseus asks Mentor, an older man in Ithaca, to look out for his family while he is away. Mentor is a proxy of sorts, especially chosen to be a guide for Odysseus's son Telemachus.

But it's not until the Goddess Athena possesses Mentor's body in order to educate and assist Telemachus that the young man comes into his power.

I was thirty-one years old before I found someone to call my mentor: Judith Tannenbaum. My guess is Judith knew this origin story of mentoring, but it feels especially right to infuse our story with Goddess energy.

* * *

I met Judith when I was a teaching artist at the San Francisco WritersCorps program, where she was the training coordinator. The title training coordinator gives me the same feeling as learning that Mentor was possessed by Athena—it is a small and mortal title that was filled by someone whose care, experience, thought, and power went far beyond the words.

In thinking about my relationship with Judith, this etymology from an epic poem feels right, as the concept is not a fixed one, but one open to interpretation. I see Judith as a gentle guide in my life. But what is most powerful was how my relationship with her transformed into a deep and lasting friendship based around the idea that unleashing and guiding creativity might just change the world.

* * *

After graduating from Oberlin College, I moved home to Dayton, Ohio, for the summer and interned at the *Dayton Daily News*, but I found I was more interested in poetry and storytelling than the life of a beat journalist. I decided to head west to San Francisco and envisioned a bohemian life of writing and freelancing and gallivanting around the hilly streets of the city, but when I got there, I couldn't figure it out. Picture me, looking out the window of my Richmond District studio at the fog rolling over the Marin Hills, feeling as lost as Telemachus did. Moving across the country at twenty-one years of age is exciting but ungrounding. The pages of stories I had written in Ohio felt flimsy and unconnected to my new life. Also, I didn't have the connections to be a freelance journalist.

I found a job at *Asian Week*—the nation's only Asian American news weekly—where I covered local and national news. At my six-month review, the editor in chief was so eager to jump ship for another job that she promoted me and left— just six months before 9/11. It was exciting to report about those tumultuous times. I was an unapologetic activist and leftist, who questioned everything and wasn't afraid to publish editorials questioning who the real terrorists were, especially in the days of the War on Terror and immigrants via the Patriot Act. I learned many hard lessons about running a newspaper, media, and managing a staff on my own. I didn't have anyone to guide me, only the newspaper's publisher, who would take me to expensive lunches and ask me strange rhetorical questions, and then eventually fire me for being too radical.

Those three years of running that newspaper and raising my voice against the Bush administration were exhausting, and left me wanting to walk away from news media. I applied and got into the MFA Program in Fiction at San Francisco State University—remembering that I had come here to tell my stories. But then I met Kevin Weston, who had built a multimedia youth media program at the storied media nonprofit Pacific News Service. He was looking for a managing editor, and I couldn't resist the opportunity, so I decided to do both.

YO! Youth Outlook Multimedia was a place where young people from all over the Bay Area could tell their stories. They were kids from the suburbs of Danville to the streets of Hunters Point, kids coming out of juvenile hall or incarcerated, young men returning from the Iraq War who already had gunshot wounds from their lives in Oakland's "Murder Dubs"/East Oakland. At YO! they could tell their stories, in their own way— through a magazine and website, a radio show, and a cable access television show.

Kevin hired me because I knew how to run a newsroom, and he wanted me to share my knowledge with the young people. I had never worked with youth before, especially those inside or coming out of juvenile hall, but Kevin believed that I would be good at it, and I was. I spent half my time in our downtown San Francisco offices, working with young people, and the other half on the other side of the city, learning about story structures and having my own fiction workshopped.

Kevin would go on to become one of my best friends, and along with the other staff and former youth of YO!, we spent a lot of time outside of the office—and sometimes inside it— drinking and partying, and also talking about the work. Kevin was notoriously cryptic about the best way to do your job. He believed in getting out of the way so people could do their best work, and he spent a lot of his time fund-raising and meeting with funders. Often, he would give me advice by referring to Octavia Butler stories and narratives, which I never quite managed to parse, but I think he was just ahead of his time. Still, he bristled when I called him my boss, much less a mentor. I think he operates more like Zeus in my story, someone who created the universe that I was able to thrive in.

* * *

After six years of working at YO!, and one year after finishing my MFA, I felt pulled to get back to focusing on creative writing. This is when I got the job at WritersCorps, and found Judith. I distinctly remember walking into the full-day training sessions that kicked off the year, how much care and thought Judith put into each step, how we had time to talk about where our own creative practice and interests intersected with how we could guide others, especially young people who may have faced trauma.

I began working at Ida B. Wells, a continuation high school in San Francisco's Western Addition. It had been around for a long time, and had large classes of students sent there because they had been kicked out of other schools. It was a challenge to get their attention and give them tools to share their stories, but I had breakthroughs, such as asking them to use Brian Turner's poetry about being a soldier in Iraq as a model to write a survival guide about their own lives. I was also placed at the San Francisco Youth Guidance Center, where I played students Nas and Alicia Keys on my tinny iPhone speakers. I asked them how they would rule the world, and what their utopia would be, and then made posters of their poems to decorate the classroom walls.

For the first time in my working life, I found a space where my holistic self was represented—my interests as a writer, a teacher, and an activist—and Judith was there to offer even more support, to ask how it went and to think through problems with me. To ask us to share about what to do when students put their heads down instead of writing, or to ask us about our own work, and how it felt to find the time to get back to it after a hard week. Judith's own experiences teaching inside of San Quentin inspired me, especially at that time. *Disguised as a Poem* became an important touchstone for me, as she wrote so clearly about the heartbreak of going inside prisons and other institutions and creating a space for art.

I only spent one year at WritersCorps, as my husband and I got an opportunity to move to India—where our parents are from—for a year. I wasn't ready to leave Judith and the special relationship I had begun building with her, and we both promised to keep in touch. Judith and I began corresponding that year, and writing to her—even across the world—let me access the same care and guidance that I'd found working with her. It was the first time in a decade that I was not juggling multiple jobs and school and projects, and I was excited to sit and think about what to do next, both with my own writing and my career. I found myself often turning to her in these moments.

Here is an excerpt from an email from August 2011:

Dearest Judith: It is around 2 p.m. and I'm at the beach in Goa, having a fresh lime soda—the most thirst-quenching drink ever. Where I am is called Patnem Beach and it is one of the southernmost developments in this Indian state, still marked by its some 500 years as a Portuguese colony. It's a sleepy little curve, the Arabian Sea warm and gently rolling. Such contrasts! India is full of them. Here in India, I'm also slowly making some connections. I found, randomly, on a shelf at the bookstore at the Jaipur Literature Festival, a book about the juvenile justice system written by the son-in-law of Kiran Bedi, the first female police officer who was put in charge of one of the biggest prisons in Delhi and starting a lot of prisoner rehab programs like the famous Vipassana program. I hope to connect with her foundation in Delhi next month. I am also planning to try to connect with a Theatre of the Oppressed group in Kolkata, since I think straight "creative writing" won't work with these populations in India because of the literacy levels, so I think I would need to focus on storytelling in a different way.

* * *

I went on to tell Judith that I wanted to apply to Ph.D. programs in creative writing, and that I wanted her advice. She wrote back within the week. Rereading this now, she comes across so strongly, as she always did in her writing: her politics, her sensitivity to the world around her, and, of course, her ability to see me and my strengths, as well. Judith wrote:

> Honestly, I don't really know what's best to do in order to stay with, go deeper, make more in community arts. I do worry that WritersCorps is so top-of-the-line (specifically in terms of pay, benefits, working conditions, etc. for our teaching artists) that there's nowhere to go when folks leave. Most don't really stay in the field exactly, though a large number do keep teaching in some way. You have multiple skills—teaching and making/administering a program—so that does give you way more options. Another reality is that it's so hard to know where this state, country, world is going (economically, politically). In the months you've been in India the force of the economic crisis feels like it's hitting full bore. Plus the Republicans. Feels totally like "the world as we know it" (a world, messed up as it's been, in which working people can make a living and in which there's been at least some attention—including funding for programs—on those at the bottom of the economic ladder) is going to be gone. Maybe a PhD would be good, allow you to be one of the

ones figuring out how we're going to do good work in the
next age.

* * *

Judith ended up writing me recommendations for Ph.D. pro-
grams, but, more important, we also began sharing more about
our own writing. I began working on a novel based on a short
story I had written during my MFA program. Judith shared her
list of writing residencies and we continued to talk about how
to balance our paid work and creative work. Along with that,
when I returned from India and moved to Los Angeles, Judith
connected me to poet and community organizer Luis Rodri-
guez. When I drove up to Sylmar, in the northern San Fernando
Valley, and sat with him, Luis invited me to join the board of his
community literacy project, Tia Chucha Centro. I also began
working at Kaya Press, an independent publishing house dedi-
cated to Asian Pacific American and Asian diasporic press, along
with continuing to be a teaching artist for at-risk youth. Judith
wrote me a letter of reference for all of these jobs, and I contin-
ued to feel her guiding Goddess energy as I made a new life for
myself in a new city.

Judith, who grew up in Los Angeles, would make periodic
trips to see her uncle and cousins, and she always made time
for a meal or a get-together with me, and I did the same when
I went to the Bay Area. When I got pregnant, Judith was one of
the first people I told, because I wanted to talk to someone who
had raised a child but still centered their art, creative practices,
and activism. Though I still considered her a mentor, the idea
became more one of mutual support.

* * *

Hi Neela, I've decided to apply for Stegner (in fiction). I've
thought about doing that before, but it seems such a wasted

effort (they take ten people out of about 2000 applicants). And I hate driving! And I don't like workshops! :) But really the application process is pretty painless and I'm just going to push myself to do it and worry about the details (driving, working) in the most remote chance I get it. BUT can I list you as recommender?

* * *

I felt so honored to be in a position where I could recommend Judith, and over the years, I wrote many letters of reference for her when she applied for residencies and grants to support her work. I also was able to share what I learned working in the publishing industry with her. As much as I enjoyed writing to support Judith's work, it was she who inspired me, continually putting her work out there, thinking and processing the world, and writing it down. I will always think of her as a guide in that way, as a reminder that whoever we are, and wherever we are in our lives, our words and thoughts and our art are important, most of all to ourselves.

After a busy few years—when on top of the work at Kaya Press, I was also teaching creative writing at UCLA—I took maternity leave in the fall of 2019. I had begun thinking deeply about writing about a death penalty case I had learned about, in which the son of the murdered man advocated for the killer's clemency. One afternoon, as I held my newborn son in my arms and thought about the angle I wanted to tell this story from, I was overcome with the desire to talk to Judith about it. I couldn't wait to send her a long email when my husband came home and took the baby from me. I started composing the email in my head. The anxiety I felt about how to tell the story suffused into a warm feeling of talking it through with my dear friend. I found out later that afternoon that she had passed away.

Having Judith in my life for a decade was truly life-altering, mostly because she showed me how to be a guide, that you can center and offer creative practices in any kind of space, and—more than anything—that being a friend means paying attention and being in touch. I know that I will always carry those ideas forward, and keep her gentle Goddess energy inside of me.

An Offering of Sky and Sea

Aracely Gonzalez

Judith is always early.

And I am always late. *The actions we take*, she says, *shape our realities and relationships.* Like many of her friends, we also walk and talk around Marina Bay Park, near her home. Like all things Judith does with heart, friendship is part of her art. Just as the water sketches the land's edge that we walk around, our words lap along with our feet and give shape to our friendship. And like all worthy adventures, we find north before setting sail: *Which is your good ear again? How long does your back have today? And your head? And yours? How much time do we have?* And though we meet through poetry, our friendship grows in the healing rituals we share in order to live in spite of pain, like these very walks and words.

* * *

Judith is always early.

Sometimes she plans to be there when you aren't. In our weekly teaching artists meetings, she arrives early to set up and patiently waits for colleagues to enter. In these meetings, Judith mentors and holds space for us to share and inspire each other so we can show up with our best selves for our students. She is there when I stumble in early, barely seeing through my migraine auras. I don't have sense enough to stay home, but I have sense enough to get an early start. As I walk down Market Street, all the smells stack on top of one another like the mismatched layers of clothes I wear to keep up with the microclimates throughout a day's walk in San Francisco: spray paint from last night's street art, fumes from the underground Muni train, fried oil and coffee from the corner doughnut shop, the lovely lady with the hair asking for change to eat, the perfume suits of pushy downtowners, the putrid cleaning of the gutters, the smelly strobing fingerprints on the elevator wall I lean against.

* * *

When I stumble into the room, Judith's wide smile turns into instant concern. Her knees and silver-brown hair bounce with the same compassion toward me. She gently holds both her hands out, places one under my elbow, and stretches the other out in front of me like a branch of stillness in a spinning world that leads me to solid ground. The slight smell of spearmint on her breath eases the turns in my stomach. She recognizes this pain well, and knows what to do. *Don't feel embarrassed,* she says like a real friend; *see, this is why I'm early today.* Waiting in a dark, quiet room for my ride, I listen to her voice through the walls, and am calmed by the steady pulse of her words as she reads poetry.

* * *

Judith is always early.

B Star opens at 5:00, but she is already sitting inside, wide-smiled, drinking water, when I arrive at 4:59. We are excited to see each other, discuss life, writing, and headaches over tea leaf salads. At times, we indulge in our pain like scientists sharing notes, thinking we might gain a breakthrough. We giggle over social corners we learn to cut in order to participate, and share strategies for strength. But soon we wonder if pain is like most things—if the more we notice it, the bigger it grows in our minds. So we talk about forgetting, and wander around water and trees and museums instead. When it eventually creeps up, by minute or by use, and it's time we can forget no more, we part ways with the joys we notice and still hold in one hand.

★ ★ ★

Judith is always early.

As usual, I'm a little late and have no way of letting Judith know, because her spirit is too free for a cell phone. We meet in the parking lot, between the memorial of Rosie the Riveter and the restaurant we'll eat at after our walk. Despite her waiting who knows how long, her smile is warm and generous, and her arms open and wide. A seagull's broad wings span over her as we hug hello, and the beauty of the sky wraps around her down jacket. We know where north is now before we meet; it grows around our limits. I know what side to stand on; she knows what times I can speak. We start our healing walk by reading words that honor strong women, the words etched in cement that leads up to the waterfront, pausing under the sky circle and small pier where we once burned words and images of heartbreak and loss and released the ashes into the windy water that insisted we work hard to let them go.

★ ★ ★

On our walk, the smell of fresh bay breeze, goose feathers, family food on barbecue pits, pies in windowsills, wild herbs, wildflowers, and spearmint, statements of all the beauty we see, delight under the chorus of seabird songs. As we walk, Judith's hands lead the way, shaping the air with the precision of her words and honest heart. *I feel good right now,* she says, pinching the sky with the twist of her thumb and squint of her eyes; she stretches back into the sparkling universe of her memories and casts out a truth, a light about the world that shimmers like the very same bright pink reflections of sunset dancing across the bay.

She shares a memory of her precious childhood and treasured family, looks out at the horizon, and traces the skyline with cupped hands. *I can still hear my father in nature and stillness.* We listen to playing kids and the quiet calls of songbirds, croaking frogs, chirping grasshoppers, leaping fish, quacking fowl, winged whispers in flight, and each other. There is no spring without women, the memorial says, and our steady steps rounding each bend agree. The walk is long but always too short.

* * *

Judith is always early.

If you arrive late, you might miss her. To miss Judith is to miss an exquisite friendship that gives love like the light of the sun. Come as a seed, and she offers all she knows to help you sprout. Come as a sapling, and she shows you the sky to stretch toward. Come as a tree, and she warms your shade with the brightness of her laugh. To miss Judith is to miss an offering of sky and sea through two precious hands that are always held open and out. To miss Judith is to miss the most delightful melody on the horizon of two blues dancing before you: the agile blue of waves strong enough to erode mountains beneath you, and the delicate wide blue, airy enough to whisper words that lift you. To miss Judith is to miss the exquisite joy of noticing the world alongside her, and the radiant colors of the sun bouncing off the bright waters of her wide-open heart.

* * *

Judith is always early.

But this time, I'm early, too, because I want to help and pick her up. We arrive before the restaurant opens, but she convinces the owner with kindness to let us sit down before dining hours in the best bay window seats of the house, just to order two appetizer salads and waters. *I'm old,* she jokes; *they can see I need to sit.* We giggle, knowing sitting stiffens and movement releases. We try not to talk about the pain anymore, even though it eats our dessert, and more and more of her salad. Instead, we look out the window and watch the sun set. The sun, she teaches me, is never early or late; it is just always rising to share its beauty on the other side. And we chew on that in the silence and stillness of the growing light within us.

At the Edge of Skin and Shore

J. Ruth Gendler

Judith Tannenbaum loved poetry, and teaching, silence, and
good talk, and it seems to me she especially loved the work of
bringing poetry to people who didn't know they could be poets
— prisoners and third graders alike.

It takes a special kind of artist to also be a committed and
generous teacher, a person willing to nurture others and help
them grow into themselves creatively and, may I say, spiritually
over many years. Judith had a deep desire to see each student
as he or she was and also to provide the guidance, inspiration,
and structures that would help each one become who he or she
more truly could be. Writing became the practice and evidence
for the process of growing students' souls. Beyond the task of
sharing the tools of poetry, Judith regarded poems as "a vehicle
for vaster understanding."[1] In a poem about what she and her
students share, she wrote, "Call it poems/call it life/call it we
breathe and we're human."[2]

When I think about Judith, I hear her voice, her cadences,
her talk filled with references to what films and art she was see-
ing, the books she was reading, and the collages she was making.
In her own poems, but also in her conversations, there was a
certain fierce searching toward clear thought, a certain ques-
tioning her way to what is true. Always walking and looking.
Seemed like whatever we were discussing, we were also talking
about courage and truth in big and small ways. Tea in her
apartment kitchens, many walks in the hills of the Richmond
Annex, or at the El Cerrito shoreline.

We met at a Poets in the Schools conference at the Oakland
museum in the mid-1980s. Judith had just left her Mendocino

village life, traveled in Europe, and came down to experience
the city with her young daughter. She was performing poems
and teaching and beginning to do the prison work that became
a huge part of her life's work. She invited me to bring my first
book, *The Book of Qualities,* to her San Quentin class. Gray sky
streaked with clouds as I walked across the large interior plaza.
Gates closing. Doors and keys. A staircase. A basement class-
room filled with six eager, urgent students who had rarely
experienced a teacher who cared about them, who didn't know
that what they wrote mattered and that language could belong
to them. From Judith they were learning they had the right to
speak and be heard.

* * *

In 2012, for her sixty-fifth birthday, Judith gathered poems
together in a book called *Carve This Body into Your Home* and asked
me to write the foreword. An excerpt of what I wrote then con-
veys my deep respect for this poet, my friend.

> Living in a noisy world, surrounded by the clamor of in-
> formation, data, opinions, advertising, bullet points and
> talking points, it is easy to forget the power of a single
> human voice. We have so many words now, and they seem
> to mean less and less. Reading Judith Tannenbaum's *Carve
> This Body into Your Home,* I am reminded what words are and
> what words do.

In Judith's poems, words illuminate our condition, point
toward the mysterious and the real, name sufferings, say what is
true. Rooted in the language of the body—*spine, small of the back,
throat, chest, toe, heel* and the language of the earth—*rock, cove, bishop
pine,* the creeks and trees of Mendocino County. Judith Tannen-
baum's language is ordinary, and yet takes us extraordinary
places, often to the edges where the inner and outer meet—the

boundaries of skin and shoreline, the doorways and entryways that we almost don't see.

Judith's poetry is a poetry of places and spaces, interior corridors, and real landscapes. Alert to the way things are not what they seem, the way "anything can happen, but mostly it doesn't," there is room for the intimate and the immense, the way that in sleep "we'll be shaped by chaos/connection. / And tomorrow wake into what night and the rain, / our words and our wonder, have made of the world and of us."

Standing at the edge, walking with questions, talking over dinner with family, waiting by the open door, resting on the ground, breathing in the light and the dark, these poems become prayers—at times hesitant, other times fierce with yearning and ache and appreciation . . .

Judith's fidelity to her experience, her tender detachment and her precise observation give these laments and praise songs their strength, their shape and power so that they become a balm, a gift to us, a present made from silence and language and courage.[3]

* * *

Caught up in the losses of two of my most important people in November 2017 and 2018, I didn't realize how frail Judith was becoming. I was taking my own journey through the grief lands and thought I would reconnect with her when I was less shattered. In December 2019, when I found out she had died, I couldn't quite comprehend that she was no longer in the world.

Searching through our last emails, I found an exchange from six months earlier, postponing a walk. I had written that although I felt like I was emerging, I seemed to be crawling back into my shell. She wrote that she was having some difficulties, too.

I am surprised when I'm driving near her apartment in
El Cerrito or when I come home with a wonderful batch of
poems from fifth graders or I think about going to a movie at
the Berkeley Museum how much I'm in a conversation with
Judith in my head.

In the last few years of learning things I didn't really want to
know, I have discovered, again and again, that grief can coexist
with delight, a reality I would like to discuss with Judith. And
also this mysterious way our dead are absent and present. How
can our beloved dead be so gone and yet sometimes still so close,
the invisible adjacents? Where are they? Seems our task is to
carry them inside us and then find them in the people and bits
of the world they loved. Why do we even say "grief," singular,
when the griefs are so multiple, and each one is its own and also
part of the others?

Jewish tradition offers many gifts and rituals for the griev-
ing. Perhaps the simplest is the statement "May her memory
be a blessing." May the light she brought to us continue to live
within us and shine out from us.

Truly, Deeply, Madly Understood

Amy Friedman

I knew Judith for nearly a quarter of a century, though during the first twenty years, we did not meet in person. We were introduced by Nancy Lord, like Judith an exquisitely clear-eyed, tender-souled writer. It was 1993. They were in residence that spring at a Virginia artist's colony where some years earlier Nancy and I had met.

"Judith is a brilliant poet and an incredible human being," Nancy told me. But then she made a connection between Judith and me that saved if not my life, at least my sanity. "She taught poetry at San Quentin . . . and she knows what prison's all about."

Nancy knew that, one year earlier, prison and its poisonous politics and the possibility of poetry had become the central focus of my life.

Back then, I lived just outside of Kingston, Ontario, a city on the eastern edge of Lake Ontario known for its beauty. But the longer I lived there, the more aware I became of something else: the abundance of prisons, both within the city's boundaries and just outside. There were still more of those sprawling edifices just across the river, in upstate New York.

I was working as a newspaper columnist with the luxury of writing fifteen hundred words every week about any subject. For eight years I'd been writing about lambing (I'd been a sheep farmer); artists' colonies; movie sets (I'd worked on those); and friendship and flying and teaching and surfing and dogs. And then one day a student in my college writing class asked, "Why don't you write about something important, like what goes on in the prisons around here?"

I took him up on the idea, interviewing everyone in Kingston Penitentiary—from the warden to the nurses, guards, and prisoners, to the teachers and psychologists. But as I was interviewing family members of prisoners, everything went sideways. I fell in love with a prisoner, and within a few months my whole world had changed.

That man and I married. For the next seven years, while he remained inside, and I raised his two daughters, I learned first-hand the stigma that attaches to those of us who love people who are in prison.

Judith was the first person I met who thoroughly, passionately, endlessly understood, and empathized. When we met, I was still learning, and by then she was well known for her innovative teaching at San Quentin, for her deep insights shared in books she wrote for artists working in prisons, and for her brilliant speeches on prison and prison arts. She hadn't yet written or published *Disguised as a Poem: My Years Teaching Poetry at San Quentin* or the exquisite *By Heart: Poetry, Prison, and Two Lives,* coauthored with her dear friend and cherished colleague Spoon Jackson. But she knew how prison worked, what prison did to the people who lived and worked inside, and what it meant to love them.

By the time I met Judith, my marriage had resulted in my being "laid off" from the newspaper, forced to resign from two boards, and the loss of friends and some family. Prison visits and scrambling to make a living not only for myself but for two young girls took a toll on my life. I focused on friendships with people who not only didn't think me mad but who truly, deeply, madly understood. At the top of that list was Judith. Although our experiences were different, we shared more than not, including some secrets about those experiences that I will never share with anyone else.

For seven years, while my ex and I remained married and he remained in prison, and as I helped the girls navigate their way through middle school and into high school, I woke many mornings to a stream of paper flowing from the fax machine strewn across my bedroom floor. A letter from Judith. At the sight, I always felt the jolt of pleasure I imagine a woman stranded on a raft in the ocean would feel at finding a bottle with a note tucked inside. I devoured her perfect sentences, her boundless kindness, her wise and careful understanding. I hope my letters back to her gave her some solace also, for she, too, suffered the pain attendant with loving people inside—people we couldn't bear to see hurt, and people who we couldn't bear being hurt by.

My husband was released from prison in 1998, but our marriage didn't weather the storm of the next eighteen months. Sometime in the chaotic transformation that happened with my divorce, Judith and I lost touch. But serendipitously, three years later I moved to Southern California, and she and I took up where we'd left off, speaking on the phone occasionally, trading in long trails of faxes for tidier (if perhaps less satisfying) emails. Some of my favorite moments were the days Judith mailed me an envelope with a piece of paper on which she'd typed out a quotation (gifts she sent to friends at holidays). Those sayings are tacked to the wall in front of my desk so I can see them every day. And every day when I read "Be joyful/though you have considered all the facts," I think of her.[4]

Judith and I met in person just twice. I never had an opportunity to meet her daughter or many of her cherished family and friends. But through Judith I have met so many wise and good human beings, and her early blessing of the nonprofit I started to support children of the incarcerated is the reason, I know, the nonprofit is still around, and growing.

I'm Jewish, and there is a Jewish prayer I never understood until Judith died, and I said it out loud: "May her memory be a blessing." Because it is.

After December

Box Study #2. Credit: Jim Carlson.

THIS SECTION BEGINS with "December," a beloved poem by Judith Tannenbaum in which she traces the pulse of life that beats even in the depths of winter. It continues with poems of reflection, mourning, and gratitude to mark the first anniversary of her death. The final two poems pay direct homage to her poem "December."

December

Judith Tannenbaum

Everywhere a pulse is beating:
in the straight trunk of the sequoia,
in the leafless oak,
in the sound of snow against digger pine.
A pulse: the madrone
with its smooth, pink flesh;
Orr Creek where downed redwood dangles roots;
the soil. Beating through things
and the names of things.
Black oak leaves caught in ice,
half-eaten body of the dead deer.
A pulse beating through Round Valley,
Potter Valley, Anderson, Redwood, Long Valley.
And in winter water that moves the world in rivers
named here Garcia, Navarro, Big, Russian, Eel.
All the forks of all these rivers,
all the falls and creeks and streams.
A pulse. A deep, drifting down.

The Morada

Barbara Schaefer

I
Before the majesty of the changing sky,
where light and shadows dance over the desert and mountains
with astonishing grace,

men flagellated themselves
years ago
in the name of religion,

as though that much beauty
was too much to let in, or

they failed to notice how the light glowed
and patterns flickered
across their brothers' faces, where
they, too, became beautiful and mysterious,
merging with the shifting landscape. Perhaps

their bodies were already condemned
by the Patriarch's iron cross, forcing their hearts
out to wander
in search of their souls, which probably were right there,
hovering over the awe-
inspiring vista,
taking refuge from those savage ways.

II
Today we walk on this terrain
as our evening liturgy,
from one cross to another,

as if destined by invisible spirits
whispering with open hearts,
our steps lightly
tracing memories, sometimes painful
the remnants of history
and what's not written, but
etched deep within the earth,
where the wind shifts sand
through time.

We pick rocks from the earth
silently chanting our prayers
as we place them upon the cross
where mythology has designated

but where the sky rules
We say;
Dear Creator,
let the beauty we see
permeate our being,
embrace our waking dreams
with your gift of movement
like dissolving sand
where understanding goes beyond language and
form moves within itself to become formless.

Let us love and be loved!

Judith Letting Go

Mark Dowie

Is this the way it unfolds, she wonders
My story given back to me
"In capital letters and broad headings"
Woven into tiny chapters that restructure a narrative
    surging with luminous episodes
Of passion pain creativity and kindness
Almost all of them followed
By a laughter
That will always amaze us

As love in every form
From every origin
Gathers speed against the pain
That's defined so much of her
For so long . . . perhaps too long

She begins the process

But wonders

How does one let go
When there's so much to let go of?

Rising slowly to find the answer
She holds herself steady
By reaching for memories
That nurture solace
And challenge her resolve
While cautiously crossing a room
Drenched with the poetic effluvia of

A woman in love with words

She pauses

And dials another friend
To share her decision
In words that now come easily

He weeps softly into the phone and tells her
He will never forget the day they . . .

Here then another sweet vignette
To leave on the floor with the dozen or so already cut
    loose

Will she smile as she drops it?
Of course she will.

How many will there be
When she stops letting go?

Enough perhaps to cobble together a slender memoir
About a girl whose father broadens young lives
While nourishing a family
With love she would carry deeply into her own
As a young woman who gives birth to a girl
Who becomes and remains, to the close, her best friend

About a poet who teaches her art to children and a lifer
    named Spoon

And the life mentor who taught her close ones more
    about death and dying
Than anyone they'd ever known

I'll let them add the chapters
About passion creativity children travel poetry and
    madness

While those who know and love her
Brace for the day she has chosen
And are saying to one another:

This one will be hard to let go

A Bardo Prayer

for Judith

Kate Dougherty

Love, in this lifetime
you opened to darkness.
Came Grief
bent, under her blue shawl.
You opened her door—
a chorus of humanity encircled her
and she wove in and out among them.
Single voices stepped forward to speak
singing in their own words,
refugees, prisoners, poets,
children others overlooked.
Grief heard their song.
She did not turn from them.
She did not step in to manage.
Bearing witness
all was seen
all was heard.

Came pain within you.
Came beauty around you.
Came the news broadcast
every morning
both-and-and-and
in a simultaneous seeing.
In the end
you were one being
radiating—what was it?

A Bardo Prayer

We could not name it—
your increased capacity
to give and receive
whatever, whoever
came before you
until you needed to lay
your body down and rest
to stand
and walk again.

May this prayer
give solace and guidance
like your favorite music
streaming from New Orleans
as on the floor you rested—
let it permeate
this dream.

Walk now seeing
the heart's conundrums,
the horrors, the honors
with that long-distance view
you always treasured;
now ultimate height, depth
and presence.

Fanfare, bread and circus,
always alert to seductions'
hooks and lures,
the easy word, comfort, surface lull,
happy endings offering to buffer it all.
You pass once more.

Who knows when
all suffering ends?

Dear Heart, know this,
your work and love
your grief and your delight
continue on this earth
as a beacon in the darkest dark
as darkness in blinding light.

Thank You, Judith

Marna Wolak

Judith
poet
mentor
activist
teacher
the mother of my best friend.

When I think of Judith, I remember . . .
being welcomed into her home in Albany for weeks at a
    time while I was in college
invitations to family gatherings in Carmel
witnessing her unconditional love for Sara through
    postcards and phone calls
the compassion and love one felt as she simply (and
    profoundly) listened
chocolate chip cookies and banana bread
her kindness
intellect
humility
gratitude
joy
wisdom.

Judith,
I am better because of knowing you
Thank you.

For Judith (After "December")

Roseli Ilano

Drift down deep inside
look in the mirror
reflecting
every color of the rainbow
on the pointed stems and petals of spring
and every shade of night, from the clouds
and slick concrete

As you drift down deep inside
feel the sun warming your skin
whitecaps racing to wash
grains of sand from the bottom of your toes
praying, pulsing closer
as your girl's tiny fingers circle yours, even tighter

You'll hear the drum of the seabird's
mourning song
breathe in the salt
breathe in the laughter, for there are smiles too
feel the sun, warming your skin

You can leave it all behind
just as you found it
lost in tiny fingers
just as you were found

Winter Light (After "December")

Maw Shein Win

> *Everywhere a pulse is beating:*
> *in the straight trunk of the sequoia,*
> *in the leafless oak,*
> *in the sound of snow against digger pine.*
> "December," Judith Tannenbaum

Nearing December's end
I envision your trees with their living trunks
    everywhere a pulse is beating
See you hiking in the snowy valley

A deer in winter light moves through the forest
The last time we met I sat in your clean kitchen
Your poetry books lining the walls
A small bowl of almonds & golden raisins
Two mugs of mint tea, shared words

Nearing December's end
I can hear your streams & creeks
the sound of snow against digger pine
Sense your warm presence in the woods

Looking and Listening

Jack in the Box #2. Credit: Jim Carlson.

"LOOKING AND LISTENING" begins with a poem by Elmo
Chattman, one of Judith's students at San Quentin, whose title
inspired her memoir, *Disguised as a Poem*. The following four con-
tributors reflect on the quality of presence that Judith brought
to her writing and teaching. In "A Question of Perspective,"
Kate Dougherty draws on Judith's unpublished manuscript
to explore how artists like David Hockney helped her find the
right distance—not too close, not too far—to support her stu-
dents. In "A Future with Fewer Walls and More Poets," Anna
Plemons and Jim Carlson recall Judith's work in the Arts in Cor-
rections (AIC) program in San Quentin through the lenses of

voice, space, and time. In his reflections on Judith's courage and creativity, former AIC director Bill Cleveland embraces what Judith called the "nouvella"—using storytelling techniques to orient teaching artists working in prison for the first time.

Disguised as a Poem

Elmo Chattman, Jr.

In Birkenstocks and handcrafted earrings
still living a life from the sixties
you enter this place
this dungeon
this dust bowl on the edge of the bay
where 3,000 men wait
for the sweet rain called freedom.

You walk a path from the front gate
across the garden plaza
Your pale feet step softly
Upon the spots where angry men have died
Don't let the pink and yellow roses fool you
This is not a pretty place.

Two flights down
you wait for us to come
bearing the fruits and scars of our embattled lives
disguised as poems
scrawled on bits of paper
last week
in a cell
when sleep was hard to find.

For three hours in that basement room
we are cut off
A million miles away
from your daughter and your cat
A hundred years from death row.

For three hours
we joust
we orbit around each other wrestling with words
we make love with words
we grow close
We meet in a place called poetry
one woman
and a few captured men
We speak of poems
and grasp at them like straws
until it is time to go.

Two flights up
the cool night air greets us
There are always those few tight minutes
waiting for the count to clear
and the inevitable parting of ways
We could go have coffee and speak of poems all night
but your daughter will miss you
and I must be back in my cell before ten.

It is always the same
For three hours
you or Phavia or Sharon or Scoop
manage to get close to me
only to be peeled away
like the bark from a young tree
leaving behind a little spot
bare and vulnerable
that does not want to see you go
but will die of exposure
long before you return.

A Question of Perspective

Kate Dougherty

Judith's unpublished manuscript, "Looking at Looking: 33 Glimpses," was her most comprehensive attempt to explore and express a lifelong inquiry into perception. Hers were not abstract philosophical musings, but existential imperatives that stymied, challenged, and ultimately guided her. Judith's humanity informed me profoundly; any who knew her could see that wherever she landed, she affected the world the better for it.

In preparing this article, I reread "Looking at Looking," along with her poetry, her books *Disguised as a Poem* and *By Heart,* and the collage journal she made while writing *By Heart.* I now better understand why Judith was resolutely insistent upon the exactitudes of what I was saying, how I was saying it, and where my seeing came from. How could I be so sure? Opinion? Stereotype? Assumption? Fact? Where did that fact come from? Pessimism or optimism held no sway. Neither did faith. What are we after here, and why? Why was Blake's injunction to cleanse the doors of perception so crucial to Judith?

In *Disguised as a Poem,* she wrote:

> . . . I longed to be able to see "human," whole. I longed for a vision that would allow me to see each of my students next to each individual guard, each warden, each victim of crime, each politician, each voter who was convinced that more prisons was a solution. And me, too; I was part of this circle.
>
> I sensed that what was required for such vision were William Blake's cleansed doors of perception, which allowed one to see "everything . . . as it is, infinite." In early

1986, I pinned a quote by the filmmaker Robert Bresson over my desk, and that tacked sheet of paper stayed within sight for the next three and one-half years: "Accustom the public to divining the whole of which they are given only part. Make people diviners. Make them desire it." I desired it.[1]

Judith taught poetry in urban, rural, and suburban public schools through California Poets in the Schools, and at San Quentin and other state prisons through Arts in Corrections and the California Arts Council. Funded by the Arts Council, she created a cross-age community poetry program at the continuation high school in Albany, California, and at one of Albany's primary schools. She designed a poetry intensive for gifted teenagers that she taught for nine summers at UC Berkeley. In her final employment with WritersCorps, she taught teaching artists in San Francisco schools.

Art, social justice, and community were the core, always, to her life's work. And from her center she continually questioned how she and others saw what they saw or didn't see. In *By Heart,* she reflected on how her teaching practice evolved instinctively, honed through paying attention.

Imagination is a human birthright: that's where I started. I believed, also, that imagination, and knowing how to distinguish between imagination and perception, is necessary for critical thinking. No matter how vigorously people with agendas . . . try to impose their way of thinking, a healthy relationship with the pictures in our own minds helps us to think for ourselves.

Another central belief is that our stories—the specific life we've each lived, our obstacles and blessings, the people and places we come from, our individual natures—are valid and worthy of being claimed and declaimed . . . each of our stories has value. Equally important to telling our own story is listening to the stories of others; how else will we recognize the whole we're all part of?

A third core belief: pictures, songs, stories, and dance are a direct expression of being human. We come into the world with the capacity to create and everyone—from an infant shaking a rattle to an elder half-lost in the old days—is, in some important sense, making art. . . . As I put the point in a poem about what my students and I shared in our prison classroom: "Call it poems/call it life/call it we breathe and we're human."[1]

"Looking at Looking: 33 Glimpses" investigates the three main ways we perceive: look and see, imagination, and memory, and her work opens with the powerful experience that inspired it.

In the late fall of 2013, *David Hockney: A Bigger Exhibition* took over the de Young Museum in San Francisco's Golden Gate Park. Posters, placards, and banners hung across town announcing the show. I saw these and thought: swimming pools, surface, bright light; the Los Angeles world I'd grown up in and left as soon as I graduated high school. I wasn't much interested in seeing the Hockney but one day I got on the Muni 5-Fulton and went anyway. The exhibit was massive, spread across two floors of the museum but, right from the entry, a wall of small portraits, I saw that my opinions—vague and based on so little—had been wrong.

Right, wrong, opinion. Such words turn my experience that November afternoon into a thought process. Instead, those hours were more revelation than mental revision.

. . . I made nine visits to the de Young during the two months of the exhibition. I kept returning to see the images themselves, of course. But the desire that most fueled those hour-long trips across the Bay on BART and the bus was to be astonished again at Hockney's capacity to look, to trust his own eyes, to explore and portray what caught his attention.

I've never particularly trusted my own eyes, I guess because my eyes saw what others' apparently didn't. I was two years old with what adults called an imaginary friend, six years old and so hypersensitive that my frustrated father accused me of being the princess in the Princess and the Pea . . . [At] seventeen, I was in a mental hospital for a brief time. I spent adult decades writing poems and working with others to write poems; loving movies and books that made it to no Best Seller list; compelled by a desire to remember—not stories, so much, not emotions—but light from south-facing windows, . . . leaves shadowing the sidewalk in front of the post office on late summer afternoons. And always, my whole lifetime, such a huge hunger to see beyond what was in front of my eyes; to see bigger, wider; to find the whole.

What I saw and what those around me saw seemed rarely to line up so, especially when I was young, I thought I must be wrong. But, wrong or not, I saw what I saw and couldn't pretend otherwise, not even to myself. By November 2013, more than six decades into my life, artmaking—writing poems and prose, creating collages and drawings, teaching and training teaching artists—had taught me to enter, play with, and shape what I saw. In those weeks I returned so often to the de Young, I desired to go even deeper, to follow Hockney's lead, to be bold, to write straight from the love of looking and from the love of the world looked at, to wonder, to claim and, at the same time, to raise questions.[1]

In the chapter on distance, she contemplates broad strokes versus fine detail; the panorama, the close-up; what is gained, what is lost.

Once upon a time . . . I performed poems. My poems and also poems by others, mostly Eastern Europeans and South Americans. . . . One afternoon I recited them to a high school class in San Francisco. A beat of silence after I said the last word of the last poem and then the teacher asked her students, "What did you learn?" A boy in the back row raised his hand, shook his head at the kind of teacher question he clearly found absurd, and said with a sigh, "It's going to take me twenty years to absorb what I just heard. Ask me then what I learned."

. . . After years standing in front of various classrooms, my last job asked me to sit in the back watching. I was called "trainer" and was there to observe teaching artists. Since I wasn't the one in front of the room having to hand out poems, respond to questions, be alert for a teaching window I could make use of, I saw a lot. I saw the cool morning light through the tall windows sweeping out toward downtown San Francisco and the Bay. I saw the feisty girl who managed both to flirt with and turn her back on the charming player leaning over from the seat next to hers. I saw that the boy in the back didn't start class with his head on the desk, but only pretended to sleep once the classroom teacher made a snide comment in his direction. I saw the girl in the corner who raised her hand so tentatively, no one noticed. I saw what the classroom teacher and the teaching artist—both busy working up close— couldn't see. I saw what only someone sitting way in the back, at a distance, would be able to notice.

More than a decade into the 21st century, one thing I
noticed from my perch at a distance was that kids at that
historical moment were given few opportunities to see or
think big. Even excellent teachers assumed students could
only handle ideas and information in tiny increments.
Scaffolding their resultant approach was often called: break-
ing the whole into tiny parts to support children as they
followed small step by small step. In the worst case, this
meant worksheets but, even in better than worst cases,
I watched children's eyes, minds, and capacities narrow,
watched them become too unsure to make leaps, watched
them less willing to bringing their own experience to what
they were learning.

How much, I wondered, was this constriction—the
teachers', the students'—due to a world where thought
was so often boiled down to a 140-word tweet? How
much was it due to the 24-hour cycle that keeps us in-
tently focused for a moment before the next new thing
appears? What about kids who worked jobs after school
and who didn't get enough sleep to concentrate, or whole
families so shoved against the wall economically that see-
ing big became an impossible luxury? How much was due
to the more than decade-long onslaught of No Child Left
Behind and Race to the Top, those federal education pro-
grams that so greatly reduced learning to the tiny bits that
can be measured by tests? I assumed the answer was "all of
the above."

Carrie Mae Weems titled one of her installations *From
Here I Saw What Happened and I Cried*. Wails and ululations are
what I felt sitting in the back of classrooms looking out at
our children in 2008, 2010, 2013.

. . . In a serious depression in my early 40s, I couldn't
feel joy. Still, most days, I forced myself to practice no-

ticing where joy lived: in freckles across the bridge of a
first grader's nose, in a crisp white bed sheet clipped to
a clothesline and billowing in the afternoon breeze, in a
small baby's head resting against her father's chest, in my
niece Emma's handmade thank you card in the mailbox.
Although I didn't have the energy to embrace the freckles
or breeze, I found I could recognize and acknowledge the
beauty. I was used to intense love—passion, jaw-dropping
amazement—but those hard years helped teach me that
looking well from what felt like a distance could nourish a
solid, dispassionate love, one strong enough to count on,
one that offered real support.

And yet, it's true, instead of solid support, distance
and dispassion are sometimes signs of disinterest or avoid-
ance. If we stand too close we see only the forehead of that
woman just slaughtered and not what killed her, but if
we stand too far back we can pretend that those drones
dropping bombs half-the-world away have nothing to do
with us.

From Here I Saw What Happened and I Cried. Yes and also
just where is *here*? If *here* is up close, up close is what we
see. If *here* is perched at a distance, we see more—wider,
deeper—and also less—less detail, fewer particulars: the
individual fades.

. . . Spiritual philosopher Krishnamurti and theo-
retical physicist Dr. David Bohm . . . examined human
emotion in the way a scientist examines salt, as Dr. Bohm
described. Salt isn't personal, doesn't belong to anyone;
salt simply is. The men agreed: salt is not personal, love
is not personal, loneliness is not personal, intelligence is
not personal. As Krishnamurti[2] put it, describing what the
men observed from their distance: "Grief is not my grief,
grief is human."[3]

* * *

Her central muse from the Hockney exhibit was the square
room showing a continuing Cubist movie

> that showed digital films of Woldgate Woods in East York-
> shire in each season: a scene in spring on one wall, the
> same scene in summer on another wall, and again in au-
> tumn and winter. Standing in front of any one of the four
> walls what appeared at first to be a conventional film was
> soon seen to be what Hockney called a "Cubist movie."
> Nine cameras had captured the plush, lovely Woods from
> slightly different angles and, taken together—side by side,
> on nine adjacent flat-screened monitors—each finished
> film seemed whole and also not quite solid. These "Cubist
> movies" allowed viewers to observe, not only Woldgate
> Woods but, also, Hockney asking, as the exhibit's website
> description put it, how to display multiple perspectives in
> one work of art.
>
> . . . The chapters ahead take Bresson's injunction to
> heart. They are glimpses of what we see with our open
> eyes—the physical world of colors and shapes—and
> glimpses also of inner vision: memory and imagination.
> Each short chapter explores one facet of seeing—windows
> that frame, veils that filter and hide, visual overload and
> visual desire, sunlight, shadows, correspondences. We
> move from one reflection to the next and, as the kaleido-
> scope shifts, a wider view is revealed, a "Cubist mo. . . . . .
> vie," a collage, a whole divined from 33 glimpses.[4]

* * *

On one of our last walks together through her El Cerrito and
Albany neighborhoods, she said if she had to do her life over, she
would have looked more and read less. She had no real regrets,

she confessed, but she was witnessing certain things that were catching a bit before they floated off to wherever letting go goes. She started reciting her list and we both cracked up because they were so Judith, these twinges of holding on. The two that I remember: not reading her favorite writers' next books and that at the end of her last town meeting she overheard a man speak quietly to the mayor. He seemed to have the same unusual perspective she had on the situation, and this intrigued her. She desired to know more about this conversation and how it all goes. Not *went,* but *goes.*

That last autumn, she emailed me, "Lewis Hyde has a new book out!" I emailed back, "Wow." We knew what that meant. It meant I was going to buy it and we would read it together. The wonder was that we would be reading his newest work together at the end of her life, because in 1983, Hyde's book *The Gift: Imagination and the Erotic Life of Property* was the first book we read together. The simultaneous study and consequent discussions initiated our friendship and forged our bond as artists supporting each other's work and life. And here, one of her wishes: to read the newest book of one of her favorite authors!

Together!

Little did we know the extent of this surprise. *A Primer for Forgetting: Getting Past the Past,* written by a master of in-depth, wide-ranging research, exposition, debate, and summation, was instead written in a form Hyde calls "prose collage." Within the categories of myth, self, nation, and creation, he gives brief excerpts illustrating the pros and cons of forgetting. Some pieces so sure, so relevant. Other pieces so sure of the opposite claim and with good reason. Side by side. Not to argue a point, but to give glimpses of looking at both sides of one coin. Instead of flipping the coin and declaring, "Heads, I win," the coin spins and refuses to land. In a slow-motion meditation on each piece, one can see further into paradox and perhaps glimpse into mystery.

Judith read the whole thing; I could not finish it. In those months, my emotional unsteadiness walking shoulder-to-shoulder with a friend at ease with letting go of her past, all the while allowing love and appreciation from her relationships with people and the world to exponentially expand, cautioned me to stay out of my head and remain in my heart. This was something I could not figure out with reasoning. And just as *A Primer for Forgetting* made me dizzy and was unsettling, to her it was fascinating, like some fairy godmother had struck her wand and another ordinary miracle popped up like a crocus between the cracks in the sidewalk of Yosemite Avenue on a solitary walk one nameless drear, drizzly day. And as for these multiple gifts from this "gift"? "Cosmic," she would say, laughing. "Cosmic," I would repeat, laughing in turn.

Art, social justice, and community, the common threads her warp; the myriad people, events, places, memories, experiences woven as weft. Aside from her constant physical pain, which ranged from debilitating to annoying, I would say to witness Judith's letting go was like watching many threads of a multicolored fabric fade into nothingness, an unmaking as organic as the making, but here is where she would caution me. Look carefully. Is this really how *she* was seeing? When not in the realm of poetry, I am more classically trained and tend to veer to logic and reason, building on ideas that lead to an answer. Don't make this an evenly woven fabric when it is collage; hold space for paradox. Think Jess, Bearden, Picasso. Not predictable mainstream American films, but Bresson, Fellini, Ozu. Think, *By Heart,* the two-person memoir: one chapter Judith, one chapter Spoon, then Judith, then Spoon, and when they meet, her view, his view. Not one speaking for the other while the unfolding story of friendship and the power of art reveal more than its parts.

To find the whole. *Everything as it is . . . infinite.* Before her death, I would have said to find the truth or God, and we would have wrangled around those three words. Better now, I see, looking at looking with her seeing, that the word *truth* be left out of any such conversation about perception, left out and let fall away with all its burdensome assumptions, invisible opinions, generational corruptions, multifaceted filters, cultural lore, and clichés.

Whole is fresh. The door is cleansed. Yes, let's start there. And there we would start, in the middle of our walk up a hill in El Cerrito, an occasional tree on our left and houses with front gardens on our right. A walk that would end before the journey of our investigation would find its natural silence. It is no wonder to me and yet also truly a wonder the following line from Blake should arrive from a friend/teacher as I was finishing this piece: "Man's desires are limited by his perceptions."[5]

Writing "A Question of Perspective" was my way of keeping her with me, selfish, perhaps, but insightful, and the insights she gave I wish to share. My way of divining the whole through her eyes a little deeper, a little longer. One unpublished manuscript in one small essay. A piece for sure. Pieces are good.

A Future with Fewer Walls and More Poets

Anna Plemons and Jim Carlson

ANNA: This essay is written in two voices. It is a retrospective of sorts, at least for one of us. For me, it is an attempt to honor one of my first literary idols, the work she did, and the people she did it with. For my dad, Jim Carlson, this essay is about getting the story of Arts in Corrections (AIC), and the chapter he wrote with Judith, Spoon, and others, down on paper.

We've broken the essay into three sections organized around the concepts of voice, space, and time. And so it seems fitting to use my own voice to say something about my positionality in relation to prison. I bring to this work particular race and class privileges that surely have shaped my understanding of things and my treatment inside the prison. Layered on that is the privilege of being a second-generation AIC teacher who has had the opportunity to breeze through doors that opened slowly, over years of trust building, before my time. I think this is important to say. To check my own privilege, I have tried, over the years, to develop a practice of listening to what scholars and practitioners of color have to say. Bearing in mind Jacqueline Jones Royster's reminder that it is "hard to listen for that which we do not viscerally know,"[1] I have tried to listen with an open heart and been ready to acknowledge the limits of my knowing. Even though my knowing is framed by these markers, I hope it can still be of use.

I've edited out some of Jim's first-draft musings because they felt too much like eulogy. And maybe I shouldn't have, because praise has its place, and it is within the rights of the elders to talk about the seasons and their passing. But some things are not passing away with the seasons—the cry for justice is as raw now as it was sixty years ago. And now that familiar plea rises from the darkness cast by the long shadow of the U.S. prison. So, there will be no eulogy. The work is not done. The particular human fingerprints might be changing, but I hope what follows is less a celebration of the past and more an invitation to push forward, to manifest a future with fewer walls and more poets.

Voice

ANNA: I first knew Judith as the poet who worked with my dad at the prison. I had only a child's interest in their shared work, since all I knew of San Quentin was what I could crane my neck to see as we crossed the Golden Gate into the city or what came home in the way of hobby crafts—little wooden cable cars and music box pianos. But Judith was as real to me as anything. She was a poet. I wanted to be a poet. So, whenever she was around, I got as close as I could, slipping scraps of my writing across the dinner table, hungry for her response. She was patient. And kind. She talked to me about line breaks and the shape of things, about the importance of letting our words breathe on the page.

When I think about Judith, I think about voice. I can still hear hers. It was clear, without sharp edges—water over smooth stones. Judith used her voice with care, as poets do, calling forth words from a well-tended garden, harvesting them with respect. In her own words, she talks of the privilege of sharing "poetry with previously silenced people" and those "whose voices are ignored or excluded from our larger social conversations." She says:

> When working with young children, or prisoners, or
> youth at high risk, my job has been to encourage people
> to speak, and then to listen as well as I can. Such listening
> functions as a mirror in which my students are able to see

a creative, healthy, and wise image of themselves they may not have previously noticed or had noticed by others.[2]

She goes on to say that after writing and reading aloud, the "mutual task" that she shares with her students is "to put their work out in the world, demand inclusion, and find room at the table."[3] The way Judith here describes her own mandate as an artist and a human—to make space for speaking and listening, first in classrooms and then in the public sphere—finds rich textual evidence in her work at San Quentin.

Besides describing her work as mutual, she tells important stories in *Disguised as a Poem* that demonstrate the learning was reciprocal. In the context of the prison classroom—a site Judith saw as perpetually endangered by the threat of artistic imperialism—reciprocity matters. And it often requires more humility than most teachers are willing to demonstrate.

* * *

JIM: Judith worked hard to earn the trust of institutional administrators and custodial staff. She was also successful in earning the trust of her students. However, this process was not without some painful lessons and adjustments. One lesson that she shares early in her book bears addressing. It is instructive to all of us working with incarcerated artists or other specific populations of folks with whom we do not share an automatic affinity. During a class session, she shared "Some Advice to Those Who Will Serve Time in Prison," a poem by Nazim Hikmet. The final stanza reads:

> I mean it's not that you can't pass
> ten or fifteen years inside
> and more even—
> you can
> as long as the jewel

in the left side of your chest doesn't lose its luster![4]

In Judith's own telling:

The room was silent for a few moments, then Richard
said, "That's a cold poem."

All the men nodded to confirm Richard's evalua-
tion of the poem's excellence, but when I asked them to
write about what one can do, even in prison, so that "the
jewel in the left side of your chest doesn't lose its luster,"
the men slouched, put a few words on paper, sat back,
doodled, and stared into space. My "What's up? What's
wrong?" was met by sulky silence. After more energetic
effort from me, Elmo finally said, "Who are you to expect
anything real from us? You sail in here with your hippie
ways," he continued, "wanting us to open up. You think
just your smile and your good-vibe talk are going to lead
to some deep sharing? Think again, my friend. What you
want is too easy, you have to *earn* closeness from us."[5]

She recounts that the men in class looked down at the
floor, but Elmo continued to hammer her with the questions of
"Who are you? Why are you here?" In the book, she writes about
how she spent the drive home letting "Indignation, Hurt, and
Revenge each have their say."[6] Where most people would have
cashed it in and moved on, Judith returned the next week—not
with answers—just returned, ready to earn the right to sit at
the table. She ultimately earned that place and influenced the
direction of the lives of so many seated there. Judith's experience
powerfully informs how the work inside should proceed. And,
through my tenure, I've seen the particular type of education
Judith received from Elmo that day play out across classrooms
and institutions. Another incarcerated program leader once said

it this way: "Please don't come here to try and change or fix us. Please come to create and hold space so we can do the work."[7]

* * *

ANNA: The structure of the book *By Heart: Poetry, Prison, and Two Lives,* which Judith coauthored with Spoon Jackson, exemplifies her commitment to bear witness with dignity by threading her own pain with that of her coauthor. When I read *By Heart,* I think of Susan Sontag and her critique of those of us who have attempted to shed some light on the lives of incarcerated artists, but who—despite good intentions—have not escaped the voyeurism that comes with "regarding the pain of others."[8] As long as incarcerated artists are Other, the teacher or publisher who carries their voices over the wall risks the "centuries-old practice of exhibiting exotic—that is, colonized—human beings."[9] The book that Judith and Spoon wrote carefully sidesteps such a danger by telling a story with elements both parallel and intersecting. They also wrote it twenty-five years after she first held the role of teacher and he of student. That relational context matters.

And in *By Heart,* Spoon gets the final word, reminding his reader that his strong voice will continue to speak long after his release. In describing his position, he quotes the character he played in the San Quentin production of *Waiting for Godot.* In doing so, Spoon demonstrates one of the key benefits of arts instruction—namely, the opportunity to hear the voices of others and let them tell us about our own lives.

* * *

Forging my path in life is a melancholic mixture of wonder and sadness. I am not happy, nor will I ever be happy, in prison. All I can say is that my character Pozzo said in lines Judith, Jim, Denise, and Jan often quoted during our

development of the play: "That's how it is on this bitch of
an earth." I will be released from prison one day, by a beau-
tiful real life or by a beautiful real death. In either case,
I have found my niche in life which is something not even
death can take away.[10]

In Spoon's description of his niche, we see precisely the type
of classroom outcomes that Judith worked toward—artists
who find their voice and use it to make space for themselves at
the table.

Space

ANNA: To understand how it was that Judith came to be a poet
in residence at San Quentin and to understand the depth of
that work and the space that she created, one needs some his-
tory. Arts in Corrections (AIC) began in the late 1970s as the
Prison Arts Program pilot project. It was funded collaboratively
by the California Arts Council, the National Endowment for the
Arts, the San Francisco Foundation, and the Law Enforcement
Assistance Administration. It quickly grew into an official unit
within the Department of Corrections (CDC), under the um-
brella of Community Resource Development. Its journey was
guided by strong support from key legislators such as Henry
Mello and powerful voices like that of Eloise Smith. AIC staffed
each of California's prisons with professional artist facilitators,
who then used their budgets to bring in contract artists from the
local community.

★ ★ ★

JIM: I had the privilege of working for over four years with
Judith to create an instructional arts program for men incarcer-
ated at San Quentin State Prison. I was the AIC artist facilitator:
an artist employed full-time by the CDC to design, implement,

and supervise an instructional arts program that brought professional artists into state prisons to instruct in their artistic discipline. The artists came from the community outside the walls to provide positive creative role models and bring the light of personal creative discovery to a dark community where names were changed to seven-digit numbers and human dignity was exchanged for anonymity and invisibility.

A maximum-security prison is a unique place to work. Bill Cleveland, the program administrator who hired me, likened going into the prison to going to Mars—nothing familiar, different gravity (much heavier), new language, different codes, different air. It is a paramilitary environment where nonuniformed individuals are immediately suspected by custody staff and have to earn trust and respect. And, contrary to common perception and expectation, our students were not humbly waiting for any program to alleviate the mind-numbing impact of incarceration. People had to demonstrate their excellence as artists and their integrity and commitment to teaching and mentoring.

Those who came from collegiate teaching to these classrooms moved from an environment where students paid a lot of money and assumed we were qualified to one where we had to prove our knowledge and artistic expertise to gain acceptance. Just moving in the heavy gravitational weight and breathing the stale air required a commitment to a steep learning curve. Many people just could not acquire the necessary skills to survive. But those of us who did found the community brilliant, committed, and exhilarating.

Judith first came in as a guest poet in our writing class. Sitting in on the class, I realized Judith was an interplanetary traveler and could be part of our developing community. That evening as I escorted her out of the institution, I asked her to return on a regular basis: one class per week. She quickly became an essential member of our AIC program team. After a few

months, we applied for and received a California Arts Council
Artist in Residency grant for her, which enabled her to be at the
institution for twenty hours per week.

* * *

ANNA: The Arts Council Artist in Residency grant was intended
for "professional artists to design a twenty-hours-per-week,
eleven-months-per-year program for a maximum of three years,
at a school, prison, hospital, senior center, drug treatment facil-
ity, or the like." Judith said what attracted her to the program
"was the Arts Council's description of the residency program as
'long-term, in-depth.'"[11] Paying attention to institutional struc-
tures is not as interesting as paying attention to the way writing
can revive a soul and redirect a life, but it still deserves attention.
The making of space for things to be born—particularly in in-
stitutions that are designed to diminish life—requires a close
and often tedious attention to the structures that constrain, but
can also authorize, possibility. And the future of prison arts and
educational justice requires an uncomfortable complicity from
those who choose to work within the systems they intend to
dismantle.

Judith writes, "In order to be part of the team that would
give life to *Godot* at San Quentin, I had to be more attuned to the
needs of the administration and staff. This shift from outsider to
insider revealed aspects of myself that would occasionally shock
and disturb me."[12] She had to make requests of, and learn to work
deferentially with, custody staff.

> Early on, Jim had taught me to compose the memos
> I would have to write and have signed in order to do
> almost anything at San Quentin. I wrote memos for
> classes I wanted to offer, memos for guest artists, memos
> to create and then distribute our anthologies, chapbooks,

broadsides, audio- and videotapes. Carrying memos around from the captain's office to the chief deputy warden, to the warden himself sometimes occupied the bulk of a week.

Now *Godot* had quadrupled Arts in Corrections' output of memos. One day in June, I sat in the office and—just for fun—counted the memos Jim, Denise, and I had written to date regarding the play. Still one month away from performance, I counted more than fifty.[13]

She goes on to recount the specifics of the types of items that had to be meticulously cataloged in such memos.

. . . One pair of beige pants with suspenders, five bowler hats, one pair of black lace-up men's shoes, one wood pipe (smoking), one gold watch, plus twenty-five additional items, including one wig (blonde) and one buggy whip, which, each individually, had been the subject of more than one memo . . .

At the bottom of the list were four "Items Not Yet Here But Will Be Part Of The Inventory When They Arrive: one bulb atomizer, one small tree, one large rock, one folding camp stool." This memo had to be signed by Jim and nine folks higher up the chain of command.[14]

And she ends this story with a summary of what she says she learned from Jim about the art of the memo.

Write a narrative, outlining everything you can think of—where and when the proposed event will occur; which inmates, and how many, will be involved; how these inmates will get where they are supposed to be; how custody will be provided; if people from the outside will come in, who will meet them at the gate and escort them inside; the impact on budget; what equipment will be involved, where this equipment will be stored, and how it will be moved from one spot to another; what the benefit of your request is to the institution.

"Anticipate every logistical and security concern and address it," Jim said, advising that I go to any staff likely to be involved *before* writing the memo in order to find out what their needs were. "Then," Jim warned, "make sure it happens exactly as you wrote it would."[15]

* * *

I deeply appreciate Judith's insider description of the bureaucratic weight they collectively had to lift to get a thirty-foot rope and a public audience into San Quentin for *Waiting for Godot*. It reminds me of two important lessons all prison arts teachers learn early if they want to make an impact. First, many seemingly autocratic institutions are still surprisingly human when you see them up close. Second, creating spaces for humanity inside inhumane institutions can require an uncomfortable recalibration of self to work that often feels at odds with deeply held—and usually oversimplified—notions of what and who we stand opposed to.

* * *

JIM: Judith set the bar high for all of us working with underserved populations, with people desperately needing opportunities to experience the creative process and find the power in their voices, individually and collectively. Through her passionate commitment to sharing the arts with all people, she set an expansive table with places for even the most, especially the most, disenfranchised of our society to sit with dignity and affirmation. She met her students where they were, acknowledged them as they were—not as targets for transformation but as people with voices that needed to be heard and included in the world.

Judith, like so many other people doing work inside our prison system, was opposed to the mass incarceration/no rehabilitation approach of the criminal justice system. Still, she learned to understand and operate within the parameters of the institutional community we chose to work in without ever accepting it. Elmo described Judith as a sandal-wearing hippie coming into the prison, and, in many ways, she was. But she was alert, focused, and committed to the task of helping men find their voices. She saw the paradoxes such as the beautiful courtyard rose garden outside the windows of the Adjustment Center, or "Hole," where the most violent men were held, and which was also the site of the George Jackson confrontation and killings of the 1960s, or the sidewalk that separated the Catholic chapel and Death Row.

She held those paradoxes as she also found allies in the administrative and custody staff—people who would mentor her and ultimately be influenced and mentored by her, the artist in residence. She quickly learned the chain of command and understood the person with the keys to let you into where you wanted to go was the individual at the bottom of the chain. We usually had the key holders review, or at least discuss, our proposals before moving ahead.

She was an influx of humanity at every level of an institution designed to dehumanize all its members—staff and inmates alike. Every Monday she would arrive with bags of homemade chocolate chip cookies for secretaries and administrative staff all the way up to the warden. She attended inmate banquets sponsored by various chapel programs. She helped plan and also instigated staff potluck lunches and other events. She even planned a baby shower for the birth of our third child, Peter, who now has cards in his baby scrapbook made by incarcerated artists. In sum, she made space.

And when previously open spaces became unavailable, she pivoted. When the institution went on extended lockdown after the murder of a sergeant, Judith proposed that she meet her students individually at their cell fronts, so she shadowed Lynnelle, our artist working with men on Condemned Row, to learn the cell-front process. We wrote a proposal and got it signed with administrative approval, which included the warden's signature. Judith used the change in class format to engage students in ways that a larger class format does not allow.

Most memorably, Judith met with Spoon Jackson, who prior to the lockdown had come to her evening class and isolated himself behind a barricade of chairs, never removing his sunglasses and never verbally participating in class. I had been concerned about his nonparticipation and had asked Judith if I should remove him from class. Even though he had not spoken in class, she said she thought he had potential and wanted to keep him on the roster.

After visiting Spoon as part of the cell-front program, she returned to the office totally impressed with his body of work. In talking with him, it became clear that he remembered everything that had transpired in the classroom. She was 100 percent right about a man I had misjudged. Spoon's own words best reflect Judith's compassionate insight:

> Judith allowed me to sit, listen, and absorb what I needed
> from the class in silence. For over a year, I came to her
> class in silence and with dark shades on. Judith allowed me
> to listen in the ways I needed to listen, to slowly transform
> inside. It was like setting a plant in a saucer of water to
> soak in what it needs for that moment. I do not know how
> she knew to leave me in silence, but still somehow include
> me in the class. It might be her innate skills as an artist

teacher to gauge and engage within each student their
own inner voice or artist.[16]

Spoon's recounting of Judith's approach to him as a student
highlights her deep understanding that finding a person's voice
is personal work that cannot be rushed and involves more than
handing over paper and pencil. Sometimes people need space.

Time

JIM: I did not take time to record and document the incredible
work that our team of artists was doing, but Judith did. In *Disguised as a Poem,* Judith chronicled her work and development as
a teaching artist in a maximum-security prison and, in doing so,
recorded the five-year adventure of creating and sustaining the
incredible AIC program we built at San Quentin. Her book is a
gift of memory to all of us who were at San Quentin from 1984
to 1989—artists, prison staff, and students. It should be required
reading for anyone desiring to teach in prison. Rereading the
book and reflecting on Judith's impact on my career, my art, my
family, and my incarcerated artist community always rekindle
my passion for and commitment to the work inside. Her influence has no boundaries or time limit. Judith had a huge impact during a season when art fed the power grid that kept the
creative lights on at one of the toughest prisons in the United
States. I rely heavily on Judith's text to give form to my own
memories.

* * *

ANNA: Since I was not present for the events that it recounts,
Disguised as a Poem does not activate memory for me, but it was
essential reading when I decided to start teaching inside and continues to inform my understanding of what is possible, and what
ought to be, in prison arts classrooms. I showed up in 2009 as a

volunteer teacher, hoping to extend the life of the AIC program at New Folsom Prison by "spinning the plates" that were already in the air. I knew I loved teaching writing, but I also knew I didn't know much—if anything—about prison.

Jim was no help. He invited me into the classroom and let me know that if I didn't develop a rapport on the first day, I wouldn't get invited back. (Disclosure: Our memories of this encounter differ. Jim doesn't think it went quite like that. But I know it did. And I love that we had that talk. Prison classrooms need compelling teachers who bring their best. Tragedy tourists and do-gooders can find other outlets where they can bleed their hearts.)

Judith's text seems to me to transcend time. And, in some ways, that makes sense. Incarcerated artists are master time benders, and during her teaching stint at San Quentin, Judith had a chance to practice her time-bending skills with some of the best.

Poets have often used their words to tear the curtain between past, present, and future. Prison poets learn this survival strategy early and employ it well. Spoon articulates the complexity of comprehending time and the necessity of messing with it when he describes his own process. "At twenty, one cannot grasp the depth of a no-parole life sentence. There is nothing to compare it to, other than death. . . . A life sentence does not sink in immediately. It can take seven to ten years to begin to understand. Life without parole is too big to grasp, or come to grips with, in the moment."[17] So, for the incarcerated poet, the ability to suspend, stretch, and otherwise shape time determines whether the soul survives.

And later in the text, Spoon describes the way he understands time in greater detail. "Trying to grasp a life without parole sentence was like trying to hold a forest fire in my hands, or an ocean in a tin cup. I knew I had to lose the usual sense of time. Indeed, a day, a month, a year, ten years, or one hundred years had to become a moment, a breath in the present. To keep going and growing, I had to let go of time."[18]

I think prison arts teachers and practitioners—to keep learning and growing—will also have to let go of time. They will need to step into a moment that compresses past and future—a moment where we can stand in a circle, drawing wisdom from those who have gone before and inspiration from the future poets who know nothing at all of prison because it was never part of their story, never a statistical probability for kids from their block.

But, to make that moment a reality, we will have to also live with the paradox that the existence of that moment requires a strategy, a list of demands, and a calendar with due dates. As bendable as time may be through poetry and prose, there are some things for which we do not have the luxury to wait. As Daniel Karpowitz has stated, we need to put "less people in prison and for less time; [make] our economy less punitive; and [eliminate] the stark racial disparities that mar all aspects of American inequality and especially criminal justice."[19] And so we link arms and we keep telling the truth—in classrooms, in courtrooms, and in the streets.

For people like me, who intend to be a teacher, an ally, and an advocate, the urgent work of breaking down an unjust system has to be paired with a clear-eyed remembering that no matter how many times we show up and participate, we always leave again. And as much as I have tried to understand what it is really like to be incarcerated, I cannot know. So I must always show respect and take my cues for when, where, and how to push from those who have to live in prison. In *Disguised,* Judith recounts a similar impulse to use empathy and intellect to make sense:

"I just want to understand," I told Manny. "I guess I must believe that if I pay enough attention, understanding will follow."

Manny shook his head. "This is prison," he said. "There is no way to understand."[20]

I know Judith heard Manny, because she included their encounter in her book. And for me, this scrap of conversation is deeply instructive, particularly when I read it in the context of Judith's life. When I survey all her accomplishments and the people and places in which she invested her time, I see Judith did not spend her time trying to make sense of a senseless and confounding system, but, rather, invested in relationships that sustained those inside and chipped away at the concrete.

In doing so, she threaded a commitment to arts instruction with a commitment to the development of right relations. And for that model, I will always be grateful. That is the kind of teaching artist I want to be. Once I realized that, the opportunities to do the work with an attention to relationality started showing up everywhere—chances to share the podium with the parent of an incarcerated student, or to bring a college student who never had a chance to visit her own incarcerated relatives into the prison to create a writing and drawing journal for kids who grew up like her, or, most recently, to send a favorite kids' book to the pregnant wife of a program alumnus and to hear back that he's been reading it to his unborn child. Those little relational exchanges are harbingers of a future with fewer walls and more poets. So I end with gratitude to those whose vision and commitment in days now past are making that future possible.

The Nouvella:
Showing Truth Through Fiction

Bill Cleveland

> *. . . the closest way to approximate in words what it is to*
> *be an artist coming in to teach in prison is not to list facts*
> *about the world of prison, but to try to render this world.*
>
> —Judith Tannenbaum, "Introduction,"
> *North Coast Correctional Facility: A Nouvella*

August 1989, Sacramento, California

It's a typical August hot plate of a day in Sacramento, Califor-
nia. I'm looking out of a dusty third-floor office window, gazing
mindlessly into a deep hole in the earth where men in hard hats
are laying the foundation of a new building. Despite the heat
and lack of rain, I'm thinking, Man there's a lot sprouting up in
this old town.

This is the fourth space in the past two years for our outfit,
known officially as the Office of Community Resources De-
velopment. The "Community" part of this clunky title stands
for something we at the California Department of Corrections
(CDC) call "outside." "Outside," as in the opposite of "inside,"
which represents the concrete and razor wire–clad citadels most
Californians just refer to as prisons. The California penal code
identifies these places as correctional institutions. Prisoners just
call them "joints."

As the summer simmers into the fall of 1989, there are
seventeen prisons scattered up and down the Golden State in
mostly rural, out-of-sight, out-of-mind communities. But that's
seventeen and counting. Not long ago, the CDC housed its en-

tire central office staff in one four-story office building. Over the last few years, what some have christened California's "Department of Defense" has been growing like an out-of-control virus, adding the staff and offices and institutions needed to accommodate the largest and most rapid prison building program in the history of the planet.

Community Resources, as our office is called, is what some around here think of as the do-gooder unit of the expanding corrections universe. My boss, Claude Finn, is one of ten CDC assistant directors. He oversees volunteers, chaplains, self-help programs like Alcoholics Anonymous, a few voc ed programs, and the unit that I run, called Arts in Corrections (AIC). If there were a Richter scale for Corrections' do-gooders, AIC would be off the charts.

I turn from the window to confront the overflowing message spike in the middle of my desk, hoping for some other way to start my day. My prayer is answered by the familiar ring of bureaucracy at work. It's Jim on line two.

Jim Carlson has been the artist facilitator at San Quentin Prison for the past four years. An artist facilitator is just that, an artist who is facilitating. In Jim's case, he facilitates the work of a dozen or so teaching artists at one of the state's two Level IV institutions. Level IV is Corrections' jargon for what prisoners call "hard time." And "Q," which was built in 1852, is as old and decrepit as it is hard, which makes it even harder.

Nevertheless, since his arrival, Jim, whose initial response to my job offer was "No way," has masterminded the building of an unlikely creative empire at San Quentin Prison. A fine artist in his own right, Jim teaches printmaking, and clears the way, literally, for the dozens of artists who make up his crew. It's quite a show. There's a ceramics program, cranking out pots and sculptures; a music department with dozens of classes and bands of every type; there is also a theater program; all manner of painting and drawing classes; and even circus arts, taught by members of, what else, San Francisco's famous Pickle Family Circus. Amid all this bounty, the jewel in Q's creative pantheon is the San Quentin writing program, presided over by an extraordinary writer named Judith Tannenbaum.

Given the sharp edges of the place, it is amazing that someone as sensitive and thoughtful as Judith manages to function, let alone thrive, at Q. But she does, and so do her students. This is a place where truth, beauty, trust, tenderness, vulnerability, color, sensitivity, choice—all the intangible qualities humans need to thrive—are virtually nonexistent. But in her funky little classroom, she makes these things available to her students through the often arduous journey of becoming a writer. The price, though, is the hard work that Judith demands. Those who hang in have an opportunity to tap into the perpetual-motion learning machine of art making. In the process, they become creators with a chance to own a bit more of their unique story—an act of personal agency that is a precious thing, on the inside.

After a few pleasantries, Jim says, "Judith has an idea I think you might find interesting."

When I hear Judith's voice on the phone, I can feel my own lesson coming.

"I think we need to make some art to support what we do here as teaching artists. This is more than just a side gig for them. They're coming here to do some good, but once they pass through those iron gates into this upside-down world, it can be disorienting. To simplify things, some of them just go into black-and-white mode. You know, where the artists and the art students become the good guys and the rest of folks who work here are the enemy. The ones who stick around learn better, but sometimes the hard way."

She pauses.

"I want to use a made-up prison to tell the real story of what we do. I want to fill it with inside and outside artists, and all of the conundrums and contradictions, the heartaches, and little victories we dance with every day."

"Is this a play or a musical or what?"

"No," she says, "I'm thinking of calling it a nouvella."

* * *

. . . prison is a world, a world not only of despair and lone-liness, violence and cruelty, but also a world of complex moments—a cell block at four p.m. during afternoon count, the Donahue show on almost every TV; a man in green leading a handcuffed man in blue from the lock up unit to a classification hearing, the two men joking about Monday night's football game; a woman serving a life sentence for murder, pouring milk from her lunch into a shallow dish for one of the homeless cats wandering around the grounds.

This nouvella, then, attempts to give some sense of the world we are entering. It does so by moving from the experiences of one character to the experiences of another. For prison is a world where "reality" is constantly shifting. Precisely the same event is likely to be described in quite different terms by an inmate viewing the action, by an officer, an administrator, by a visiting artist behind walls for the first time. As artists, we are trained to know about perspective, point of view—about how the whole is com-posed of individual parts.[21]

October 1989, U.S. Interstate 80

I am heading west out of Sacto. The big green-and-white sign overhead shouts SAN FRANCISCO 75 MILES. Thirty minutes later, the tiny sign for the California Medical Facility flashes by a few hundred yards before I break hard and hit the exit. Never fails, blink and you miss it. Those few who do notice that sign probably think it's just a hospital. But it's not. It's a prison.

CMF, as we call it, opened its gates in 1954 as part of a post–World War II prison-reform effort initiated by then Governor Earl Warren. Back then, the idea of prisoner rehabilitation was the newest big thing in corrections circles, particularly in California. CMF's original mission was providing long-term care for the most acute physical and mental health cases in the system. But that was then. A few years ago, the word *rehabilitation* was actually stricken from the state's penal code. Today, CMF is pretty far along in its transition from full-service hospital to a typical lock and feed institution with a larger than normal infirmary.

As I turn into the institution's parking lot, I catch sight of Judith on her way to the front entrance, lugging a big three-ring binder. Over the past few months, she has been filling that binder with transcripts of interviews with San Quentin staff, prisoners, and AIC artists. Those conversations and the stories they hold will provide the foundation for the "nouvella." But given its Level IV status, and the presence of California's Condemned Row, no one could argue that San Quentin is a generic prison, if there even has been such a thing. If the nouvella's fictional North Coast Correctional Facility (NCCF) is going to translate beyond Q, we both agreed that her research would need to broaden. CMF seemed like a good place to start.

We are met at the front of the institution by artist facilitator Jerry Meek and Community Resources manager (CRM) Joe Henry. Jerry has been here since AIC's early days. He runs a great program and has a good relationship with the CRM, who is his on-site supervisor. Based on our experience at San Quentin, we know the quality of their collaboration is an important story to tell. This is why we are here.

Judith's approach to crafting the NCCF story is quintessential, well, Judith. As a colleague and a teacher, she is both nurturing and tough. She is that way with herself, too, with a marked emphasis on the *tough.* To her, writing well means pushing, digging, questioning assumptions, challenging conventional wisdom, and paying attention to detail.

That said, the novella poses some unique challenges. Most of Judith's writing has consisted of works of art, poems, and stories crafted painstakingly in her unique voice, expressing what she wants to say, freely, as an artist. Compared to this, our nouvella is the writing equivalent of a straitjacket defined principally by the fact that she will be creating an official document for the most paranoid and restrictive bureaucracy in the state.

But, of course, Judith loves the challenge of testing herself in uncharted territory. As an artist, she also understands that she has to be true to her own well-honed creative processes. This means immersing herself in the subject matter and opening up to the widest range of possible characters, stories, and plot lines. As challenging as the project is, she knows she can't begin by obsessing over the inherent restrictions. She also knows that she cannot convey the fractured logic of the prison sea from a singular perspective. All of her central characters will have to speak for themselves, interpreting each scene from their own perspective.

After our CMF visit, Judith's research takes her to three more institutions. The innocuously named California Training Facility (CTF) is a Level III facility plopped in the middle of a lettuce field in the San Juaquin Valley. Because it houses a large number of gang members and has a long history of violence, CTF is also known as "the Gladiator School." The second is a Level II facility nestled in the Sierra foothills, appropriately named the Sierra Conservation Center. The third is the state's only women's prison, the California Institution for Women, near Ontario.

By December, Judith has settled on the cast of characters whose lives will be bound up in the North Coast story. In addition to artist facilitator Al Greer and CRM Delores Mendoza, the institution's writing program features prominently, with veteran instructor Susan Robertson and a visiting poet named Varella. Although they differ in many ways, Susan is quite obviously Judith's North Coast counterpart. Varella, Susan's good friend and poetic partner, brings an unvarnished outsider's perspective to the story. The highest-ranking administrator is Delores Mendoza's boss, Associate Warden Sam Randle, who, despite a couple of decades climbing through the ranks, approaches his job with brains and a heart. Correctional Officer Betsy Chin follows suit from her own position as one of a small number of women COs trying to make a decent living in one of the most testosterone-saturated workplaces on the planet.

Naturally, there are a number of prisoners with central roles. These include two talented and outspoken prison writers who figure prominently in one of the novella's most intense episodes. Mitch Reiser is a brilliant poet and painter, whose devotion to the writing program goes far beyond his love of writing. Another writer, Timothy Augustus, is an uncompromising soul who very much keeps his own counsel. Timothy understands that the distance you maintain between what you know and what you say can mean a lot inside.

$$\star \; \star \; \star$$

North Coast Correctional Facility
(Writing Program Classroom)

Mitch was a subtle one, although Timothy had to laugh and laugh to himself at how the observant poet Susan seemed so oblivious to what to him was so obvious.

Or, not exactly oblivious. Clearly uncomfortable. Timothy could see that Mitch was interpreting the way Susan tugged her hair, looked away from his gaze, as a statement that some part of her wanted him, too. Mitch was reading Susan's vulnerability, her inability to draw a firm line, as a sign that eventually she might be his.

Eventually. That's what Susan didn't quite get. Timothy knew that Mitch had all the time in the world. He was a lifer; he wasn't going anywhere. He could approach her with his love poem, watch her get to a point of maximum confusion, then pull back, throw out something a guest artist said two months ago, talk about a poem Susan once read, refer to the way Tall Tony recited when they made the videotape. That slow build-up of shared details was bound to make someone like Susan feel safe.[22]

* * *

December 1989, San Quentin State Prison

San Quentin is our biggest program and nearby, so I get down there a lot. Hitting the road at 5:30 A.M. beats the traffic and gets me across the Richmond–San Rafael Bridge in plenty of time for my 8:00 meet-up with Jim and Judith. After I park, I grab my briefcase and head for the single-wide trailer that serves as the first checkpoint for entrance into the facility. The CO on duty passes me through with the flash of my CDC ID.

Every time I come here, the incongruity of the bayside bump of land known as Point San Quentin truly overwhelms me. On my left, mewing gulls rise up against a cloudless blue sky stretching above a fourteen-mile expanse of the San Francisco Bay and the city's iconic skyline. On my right, a mortared castle right out of *Macbeth* looms, sans the maces, moats, and moving trees.

As I approach the twin castle towers that frame the institution's main entrance, a green cluster of first-watch COs spill out on their way to the staff parking lot. The last one out nods and holds the heavy iron door for me. It's a cliché, but it really is like passing through the portals of hell. Inside, day fades to gray and the bay sounds are smothered by the hard metal clicks and crashes of the sally port gates echoing in the entryway's vaulted stone passageway. If anyone needs a reminder of where they are, this medieval tableau should leave no doubts.

Across Q's central courtyard, the square squat Education Building is dwarfed by the five-story housing units on either side. As I enter the door of the AIC office, I am reminded of how precious space is in here. Jim's basement lair is more like a closet than a real office, more so because it also functions as the AIC storage locker. Sitting among boxes of oil paint and art paper, Jim and Judith are engaged in an animated conversation. They each smile in my direction without breaking the rhythm of their back-and-forth.

"It's a work of fiction," Judith is saying, "but it has to be grounded in stories that are true. No fabrications, no cutting corners—that's where real trouble lies. Everybody here knows what went down."

I hadn't been tracking the conversation at first, but now I understand. Judith is talking about how seemingly innocuous things can become a big problem in a hurry. The need to be friendly but not friends.

"It's one of the most important and least understood lessons our people need to learn," she says. "It has to be in the nouvella. And I know this story better than anyone."

I know what she wants to do, where she wants to take the nouvella. Once again, I am struck by Judith's courage.

★ ★ ★

North Coast Correctional Facility
(Unit 3, Third Tier)

NCCF is on indefinite lockdown following an inmate stabbing. Because of this, writing instructor Susan Robertson is working with her students through the bars of their cells. She approaches Mitch Reiser's cell.

"Hello, Susan. Coming this way?" Mitch Reiser's voice broke into Susan's thoughts on violence and its effect on the mind and soul. She walked past a few cells to where Mitch was housed.

"Are you psychic or what? How did you know it was me?" Susan asked, always on her guard with Mitch.

She was never able to be herself with Mitch around. And Mitch was always around. There were so many silent ways in which Mitch made sure he was there, always there.

"I am psychic where you're concerned, but this time I have to give credit where credit is due."

Mitch pointed to the small mirror that he could adjust to give him a reflection of just what was coming along the walkway. Susan stepped back and looked at the other cells and saw that many such mirrors were now focused on her.

She shook her head, "I'm a trained observer, but I'm not seeing anything well today!"

"You may not be seeing well, but you sure are looking good."

Susan smiled, "Cute. Corny, but cute."

This parrying with Mitch was easy, but dangerous. If she wasn't careful, he'd pick up whatever she said and run with it as far as he could.

"Susan, come closer."

"I can hear you fine."

"But I want to smell your perfume."

"I don't wear perfume," she said, then thought, Shit, he's trapped me. I've got to get out of this dialogue without one more personal exchange.

"Then why do you always smell so sweet?"

"Mitch, what poems are you going to read at the banquet?"

"I don't want to talk about poems."

"That's what I'm here for."

"Does your husband give you flowers?"

"Mitch . . ."

"I'm going to send you flowers. You'll see. Sometime you'll be home alone, night will be coming on. Maybe you'll be taking a bath, or rubbing oil over your naked skin. And they'll be there, these surprise flowers. And you'll know they're from me."

"Okay, Mitch; that's it."

Never had the promise of flowers sounded so like a threat.

"I'm going to love you forever," Mitch whispered toward Susan's departing back.

Although she tried not to hear, she heard, "I've got all the time in the world, Susan, and I'm going to take as long as I need to convince you. And I'll convince you, you'll see."

A bird had flown in through the open transom and
was singing in the block; Susan focused on this bird.
Its song made her hear the weighted silence of the gray
sky outside, the ocean water; she listened to these silent
sounds that rode under her quickly beating heart, under
all the noise in the block. She wanted to leave Unit 2, run
back to the office and talk to Al about Mitch. But she de-
cided to see the rest of her students first, and she walked
down the tier. As steady as she could . . .[23]

* * *

Judith's act of courage is, of course, her willingness to share a
fictionalized version of a similar struggle she had with one of her
students. Like "Mitch," this poet, a lifer, with two rape-murder
convictions, was a persistent edge pusher whose obsession with
Judith became more and more tenacious over time. The line was
crossed when a staff member overheard him describing in detail
his plans for Judith to fellow prisoners.

This was a terrifying situation for Judith. And, because of
the program, other women at Q, the rules, and a dozen other
reasons, both paranoid and real, the incident could not be writ-
ten off. Her conflict about reporting it up the chain of command
only added to her distress. Her compassion in telling this diffi-
cult story in the nouvella is a testament to the enormous sense
of responsibility she carried for each of her students.

Beyond the episode with Mitch, the North Coast story un-
folds with other unsettling twists and turns, all of which are
based on the true events chronicled in Judith's research. In ad-
dition to the fatal stabbing and subsequent lockdown, there is a
discovered tryst between a yoga teacher and a prisoner, a crip-
pling state budget freeze, and, most devastatingly for the arts
program's teachers, students, and their families, the cancellation

of the first-ever arts program banquet, which had been months in the making.

Despite the intensity of this string of events, Judith's narrative is not overly dramatic, and pointedly so. This is because one of the most incongruent characteristics of prison life is the plodding drumbeat of hard-to-imagine juxtapositions—boredom and fear, cacophony and silence, bad news and no news. If the joint could talk, it would surely be shouting, "You think you caught us at a bad time? Nah, this is normal. You think this is crazy? Wait 'til next week!"

As daunting as it might seem, Judith understands that her principal job here is as a translator—making some sense of a place where the Queen of Hearts and the Mad Hatter would feel quite comfortably at home. A place where seemingly simple questions about the "right" thing to do are answered with alternating layers of clarity and quicksand. A place where the signs and signals we all depend on to find our way are offered up in a "Yes/But No" way, an oscillating current that is both confounding and oddly thrilling. Who else but an artist could render this world in a way that both attracts new creative colleagues and discourages the slakers? Her task is to convey the elusive truth of this foggy netherworld without scaring away the potential pathfinders.

* * *

North Coast Correction Facility, Susan Robertson's Classroom

Truth. Everyone in this place was always so sure of his opinion, from Sam Randle to Dolores Mendoza to Roger Watson to Timothy Augustus. Susan moved through NCCF from one whole truth to the next and in the moving, everyone's truth became part of some larger truth. It was this truth she herself was most interested in, although it was so large, she couldn't see it, didn't understand its shape. She felt she could never know prison, never understand harm to others or feelings of retribution or society's inequalities or spiritual evil or human greed or moral laziness or being a good soldier, without getting some glimpse of this larger picture into which it all fit.

She felt Timothy Augustus' observations about dominant white society were accurate, but they left out Sam Randle's ideas about individual responsibility.

She felt Sam Randle's ideas about individual responsibility were valid, but they left out Tall Tony's knowledge of how The System set things up so that the individual hardly had a chance.

She felt Tall Tony's knowledge was precise, but it left out Dolores Mendoza's experience of becoming part of The System in order to break out of a past that wanted to limit her and her people.

She felt Dolores Mendoza's experience had much to teach, but it left out Woody sitting in his cell focusing not on culture but on the clear strain of a voice that could only be heard when all was quiet, a voice that asked him to be a channel for its words.

There was a larger picture, she was sure of it, but maybe she'd never see it whole, maybe she'd always be able only to listen to each person's story, each person's way of perceiving the world.[24]

★ ★ ★

There is no doubt: Susan Robertson's yearning for some kind of whole truth nags at Judith, too.

But, of course, Judith does have access to a kind of truth that most people living and working in prison never encounter. There are true things that emerge every time she sits down with her students, shuts her eyes to the fluorescent glare, and listens to them read. There are profound things that jump out at her every time she looks in on the painters and the R&B band and even the jugglers, every day making their depleted world anew. There are the astonishing things she hears over and over when one of her fellow teachers shares a story about what happens when an individual soul is reacquainted with the power of imagination.

★ ★ ★

North Coast Correctional Facility (Music Room)

"And Gordon (the guitar teacher) told us all a story tonight that's kind of been staying on my mind," T.J. said. "Said when he first taught in prison it was down south and he was teaching a beginning guitar workshop. All these dudes hardly knew the fingerboard from the sound hole. Then this one brother walks in, picks up a box, and starts playing righteous progressions, elaborate work.

"Gordon listens a while and then approaches the man, says, 'Your playing is mighty fine, but this is a beginning guitar class.'

"'I am a beginner,' the man says. 'This is the first time I ever picked up a box.'

"'But that's impossible,' Gordon argues. 'You're playing chords and progressions

and . . .'

"'This is the first time I ever picked up a box,' the man repeated. 'Thing is, I was locked up at Central State. In the hole for ten years. No guitar, no nothing. I got me a chord book, though, and made myself a keyboard out of cardboard and just went through the book. Done with that one, I found myself another; did that the whole time

I was down. But this is the first time I'm hearing how it sounds.'"[25]

* * *

In early 1990, eight boxes, each containing twenty copies of *A Manual for Artists Working in Prison,* are delivered to the AIC offices in Sacramento. The second page imprint reads "Published by Arts in Corrections—Printed by the Prison Industry Authority (PIA)." The PIA is one of dozens of prison "industries" operated by the CDC using prison labor. Given the thousands of prisoners involved in AIC, it is quite possible that some of them also took part in its printing.

By spring, all but a few copies of the manual have been disseminated to California's now eighteen prisons, where they are put to use orienting new artists ("the fish") swimming in from the outside.

Legacy

LWOP (Life Without Possibility of Parole). Credit: Jim Carlson.

The final section examines the legacy of Judith Tannenbaum. It begins with her poem "Spoon Says to Write Reckless," whose title reaffirms how she received as much from her students as she gave. Katie Adams has written a personal testimony of Judith's role in creating the Prison Arts Coalition (PAC) in the late 1990s. Wendy Jason picks up the story, recounting how she drew on Judith's vision to transition PAC to the Justice Arts Coalition in the 2000s. Joseph Lea offers his own memories of Judith's catalytic role at prison arts conferences and of the friendship that inspired him to endow the inaugural Judith Tannenbaum First Time Entrant Award for Poem in HM Prison Dumfries, Scotland. Finally, in a "letter to her future self,"

Tiffany Golden, inaugural recipient of the Judith Tannenbaum Teaching Art Fellowship at Chapter 510 & the Dept. of Make Believe in California, exposes the vulnerability and "recklessness" that were at the heart of Judith's life and work.

Spoon Says to Write Reckless

Judith Tannenbaum

The redwoods stand close by the river.
Sunlight and shadow, gravel and rock,
stumps, some fine sand.

A small child wraps her legs around fiber,
pushes off from the bank on this swing:
Arched spine, head leaning backward,
long loose sun-greening hair.

The river is high after spring rains, runs rapid.
Her bare body through air into water
early summer, late morning cold. Heart
tightens with that plunge to the bottom.
Sand shifts through toes, tickles her feet.
Nothing solid to stand on so she sinks
and then leaps, kicks, and splashes. Those
fisted fingers now freed from frayed cord
fling wet reflected upside down dappled world.

Space Worth Fighting For

Katie Adams

Several months ago, when my friend Spoon Jackson approached me about the idea for a book filled with dedications to our friend Judith, I was first thrilled and then paralyzed. My resounding "YES" came from the knowledge that the world owes Judith Tannenbaum a lot. The paralysis came from persistent grief and my own failures with language. Lots of people in this book have different things in common with Judith, and, like Judith, have worn many hats over many years in the work that we do. Of all the roles I have in common with Judith, our friendship really took shape around our understanding as teachers and poets. Her laughter and curiosity were infectious and her love and understanding comforted so many.

On any given day, then and now, my dialogue and debates with her continue. Whether through email, phone calls, or walking through Berkeley or on the Blue Ridge Parkway, Judith always had time and patience for one more discussion, rebuttal, and consideration.

"But what if we looked at it this way" was a phrase that often bounced back and forth between us. Every time I have turned to this piece, my dedication to Judith, those words come back to me. I can almost hear her disagreeing with me and not wanting the focus to be on her.

Over twenty years ago, before the Prison Arts Coalition, there was what Judith called the "Blue Mountain Group." This was a gathering of teaching artists from all over the United States who met at the Blue Mountain Center in upstate New York in 1998 and 1999 to address a growing crisis throughout the prison arts and education world.

We were meeting on the heels of Clinton's signature on the 1994 crime bill, the loss of Pell Grants for college students behind bars, and the complete collapse of most education programs (and often related arts programs) inside prisons. By 1995, those programs dropped from over four hundred to five.

The weekend of that first conference, close to seventy-five people gathered with this crisis in mind. It was there that I first met Dick Shelton and Joe Bruchac, who together had almost eighty years of experience teaching writing in prison. I was familiar with Dick's work with Jimmy Baca, and Joe was a legendary storyteller, writer, and editor who had smuggled poems out of places like Folsom Prison during times of deep unrest and published them.

That weekend was also the first time I met Judith in person (we had already established a friendship on the phone and via email). It was also a first for connecting with key artist-educators like Bill Cleveland, Stephen Harnett, and Buzz Alexander. Everyone had a range of experiences, but we all came with one goal: How can we nurture these connections, focus our efforts, and grow as a movement?

A poet and teacher in my twenties, I had been teaching inside prisons for about five years. I brought to the table an odd mix of academic, nonprofit, and prison experience. I was teaching creative writing inside Sing Sing prison and directing the YMCA's national Arts and Humanities program out of my tiny East Village apartment in NYC. I had also just founded a nonprofit that produced a literary journal, *Prisonerswrite,* which published writing and art by incarcerated artists. Our first issue came out right before Judith's first book, *Disguised as a Poem,* hit bookstores nationwide. Right before that weekend in upstate New York, Judith and I had completed one of many mutual assignments, reading them over a second time with these future questions in mind.

We spent two full days in conversations and collaboration around a single question: What future do we dream of for arts programs in prison? What are the first steps?

That weekend, conversations took shape around making the arts accessible to everyone inside prison and what that future and structural support might look like. Each person came with stories about prison and they all came with a connection to Judith.

* * *

There is a lineage and hierarchy in this country in almost every discipline. Knowledge is like real estate. For years, I thought academics were the keepers of that precious real estate we call literature (produced anywhere), but really, all along, it was the poets who knew, understood, and protected language.

When it comes to art, education, and the history of literature created inside prisons, most academics and nonacademics defer to H. Bruce Franklin, former American Studies scholar from Rutgers University in Newark. I remember racing through the hall at Columbia University during the first Critical Resistance Conference in 1999, looking for Bruce. It was unusual for me to seek people out in this way, but Judith felt strongly that I needed to know him.

So, that weekend at Columbia, I did two things: I sold T-shirts and I found and met Bruce Franklin. Later that year, Bruce and Judith agreed to be on my doctoral committee. But it was Bruce who, in emails and meetings, reminded everyone on that committee who the expert was—the poet who had spent a lifetime smuggling poems into and out of prison: Judith, "the Poetry Lady," a title she acquired almost everywhere she went.

One hot July day, during a weeklong visit to North Carolina with my family, Judith sat in a classroom in a youth facility where I had taught in the mid-1990s. Foothills Correctional

Institution is a "closed facility," which is like a maximum-security prison in New York State or a Level III prison in California. When I had taught there, my students had been between seventeen and twenty-five years old. It had been some time since I had been back inside this prison. I did not know the group we were meeting with that day, except they had all just started community college classes that summer in the prison.

I have gone into many prisons over many years, and have taken many inside for special events. Foothills will always be significant because it was my first time inside a youth (not juvenile) facility and almost all of my young students were lifers. Many of these "kids" had been locked up since they were ten or twelve years old. At eighteen or nineteen, almost everyone had given up on them.

Judith did what I knew she would do. Through her presence, the questions she asked, writing prompts, and in stories, she transformed the space of that prison classroom. She challenged their assumptions, pushed their boundaries, believed in their minds, treated them with deep respect, and by the end, it was just the Poetry Lady sitting around telling stories with a bunch of boys who hung on every word.

When I think of what Judith gave me and others, I remember the way the faces of these young men changed in a matter of minutes. The moment poetry was made accessible was also the moment everything about that space changed—light, color, even the air quality.

This book does what Judith would argue it should not do: It recognizes her contribution and honors her role as someone who shaped multiple movements and lifted up the lives in each. Additionally, this book does what she would absolutely demand that it do: inspire and celebrate a world filled with hope and a space where poems and poets are everywhere and in all things felt, seen, and heard.

* * *

This poem

is not about prison
or lockdown
or poets
on mental health meds
or pink stained skirts
made from bath towels
yellow T-shirts
white on black
black on black
betrayal between brothers
in the shower
in the wood shop
for crank
for fun
the SHU guard
on third shift
or rage
that can only be grown
in a box
6 by 9, 5 by 6,
or 8 by 10
the lucky ones
or 1000 push-ups a day
in a dark,
paint-peeling hole
in upstate NY
for 5 years
and 3 months
without sunlight

grass or air
the gentle
wet or dry breeze
that pushes across a porch.

This poem is not about prison
but how one swims
through a room
thick with rage
when the rain comes
on a summer day
and these mountains
start to cool.

Being Human Together

Wendy Jason

I first met Judith Tannenbaum in 2010, shortly before interviewing her for an article I was writing for Change.org about *By Heart,* her memoir with Spoon Jackson. Judith and I became friends, mostly through our email exchanges. I saw her as a mentor, and I'm indebted to her for entrusting me with the management of the Prison Arts Coalition (PAC), an online platform she developed with fellow teaching artists and friends Julia Taylor, Emily Harris, Allie Horevitz, Rachael Zudak, Jaime Nelson, and Suzanne Gothard. PAC served as a hub for those involved and interested in providing arts programming in carceral settings.

Over the last couple of years, PAC has evolved into the Justice Arts Coalition (JAC), a nonprofit with a national reach. JAC serves as a central body for those working at the intersection of the arts and justice, using the arts to build community across the walls and amplify the voices of people experiencing incarceration. JAC would not exist but for Judith's vision and trust in me to carry it forth.

I had spent most of the year prior to connecting with Judith facilitating a creative writing group at a jail in Albuquerque. Initially, it was fieldwork toward my master's thesis on the intersection of the arts and restorative justice. I kept going because I couldn't imagine being anywhere else but in the company of the guys in the group.

It was my first experience working inside, and the time was impactful. When I did finally leave to accompany my partner to D.C., I planned to launch into a livelihood doing more of the same—either as a teaching artist or with an organization focused on restorative practices.

My shiny new master's degree in Coexistence and Conflict failed to open doors, though. The term didn't mean much to most people, nor did it align with the fifteen-plus years of social services work outlined in my résumé. Feeling displaced in a city I was new to and not thrilled about living in, and disheartened after sending countless job applications into a black hole, I hadn't expected Judith to see in me something she believed in, something to ignite a creative collaboration that changed my life.

Though I derived a great deal of meaning from my work in social services, I didn't belong in that system, and was fearful of having to return to it. I couldn't stand by silently while folks who were seeking support during the most challenging times in their lives were treated in oppressive and dehumanizing ways.

I was constantly being told by superiors to keep my mouth shut, to check my boundaries, to be less emotionally involved in my work. It often felt as though I was being punished and shamed for caring. I was pushed out of a couple of these jobs because I demanded that people be treated with respect and care. Judith could relate to how much of my heart I put into my work and believed it should be celebrated.

Judith and I also shared a frustration with the commonly held idea that, as teaching artists, we were doing the work of "rehabilitation"—that the people we met in jails and prisons were somehow broken, in need of fixing, and that we, as "professionals," knew something they didn't know about how to exist in the world.

We were not in it to change people. As Judith says in her essay "Human Beings Together," ". . . change isn't the point . . . I was a person sharing with other people. To intend to change someone requires an assumption that you know more than he does. I knew more about poetry than most of my students, and they knew more about living with regret. We all knew something about keeping one's spirit alive in the midst of darkness.

We each had strengths and weaknesses, we each had done good things and bad things. We were human beings, and for a few hours each week, we were human beings together."[1]

We will never experience all that a person is unless we can be fully present with them. In the same curious, welcoming way she approached her relationships with incarcerated writers (and, probably, in the same way she approached everyone she met), Judith wanted to know me and everything that made me who I was, no matter how messy that might be, and she held every part of me with care.

Growing PAC

My article on *By Heart* was republished on the blog of the PAC website, and the PAC managers began sharing other stories I'd written for Change.org about arts programs in prisons. More than just an online resource and hub for information about arts programs and prisons, though, the founders of PAC wanted it to be a virtual space for people in the field to share resources, opportunities, and stories, and to feel more connected to one another.

At that time, the field was relatively small, but folks within it felt isolated. They had few opportunities to come together, to share in their challenges and celebrations, to give and receive support. Being someone who cares about people in prison, and who spends time building community with them within institutions that are designed to strip them of their humanity, can inevitably result in a great deal of sorrow and frustration.

Having to abide by or find ways to skirt harsh rules that go against your values about how people deserve to be treated can wear you down. The hardest thing, at least in my experience, is walking out of the gates at the end of a day, carrying the heaviness of knowing the people you've just left behind have no choice but to leave the tender space that's been created within your classroom and return to the stark reality of their lives inside. You've just spent sacred time with them in which they've opened up, taken risks, laughed, maybe cried, and now, you get to leave, and they're stuck. While there's always gratitude for the freedom you have, there's deep sadness and rage as you fully come to terms with what's been taken from them.

Most people who haven't had this experience can't relate to it. It's difficult for teaching artists (and people who offer other types of programs inside) to find folks they can turn to when they need guidance or support. Judith knew this all too well and felt how much of a difference it made to be in regular contact with peers in the field. She saw PAC as a first step toward bringing together teaching artists from across the country, while simultaneously providing a platform for the voices of the incarcerated people in their programs.

The site and email account associated with PAC didn't take long to garner attention, and it quickly became more work than the founders could manage. A few months after we were first introduced, Judith asked if I'd be interested in managing it. She knew it would be a source of meaning for me, a way for me to deepen my connection to the field. PAC had no financial structure, so she couldn't offer me compensation, but that didn't matter to me. It felt so affirming that she trusted me, and I jumped at the opportunity.

Over the years, as I developed different parts of the website, managed the email account, and increased its social media presence, I saw PAC generating more and more attention and interest. People from across the country and beyond would send inquiries: "How do I start an arts program in my local prison?" "How do I exhibit artwork by incarcerated folks?" "Where can I get information for my research?" The website had become a primary resource for information about arts programs and artists in carceral settings, while more and more incarcerated artists were reaching out to find a platform for their work.

Simultaneously, teaching artists were reflecting on the need for a central body beyond the website to keep people in the field connected and to raise the visibility of their work. At the 2015 Arts in Corrections conference in California, I joined a steering committee whose goal was to create a national organization to serve this purpose.

Judith opted out of the committee, but I felt a responsibility to make sure her presence was felt. Through management of the PAC website, I had developed connections with all sorts of people who were invested in increasing access to the arts within carceral institutions and opportunities for the creative work of incarcerated folks to be experienced by people on the outside. I felt well situated to speak to the needs of a field that was expanding quickly and included not only teaching artists but also currently and formerly incarcerated artists, individuals, and families wanting to support their incarcerated loved ones, academics, activists, and others.

As the entity imagined by the steering committee began to feel more and more like a professional association that was going to be exclusive to teaching artists, I pushed for the vision to become more expansive and inclusive—to lean into the interdependence between people inside and outside of prison who were dedicated to the work of building bridges, learning about ourselves and one another, and reimagining justice through the arts. All were integral pieces of the whole.

Becoming JAC

In the fall of 2018, it became apparent the time was right to stop talking about the Justice Arts Coalition and start building it. I'd been working for three years as a housing-program coordinator after my search for work related to restorative justice and the arts proved futile. I was volunteering about twenty hours a week to PAC—mostly trying to keep up with the huge influx of inquiries coming through the email account and letters arriving from incarcerated artists. Interest in PAC's resources had continued to grow. It felt more and more like the time was right to move forward with our plans for JAC.

The steering committee was meeting regularly and continued to talk about launching JAC, but there wasn't a plan of action. When I learned that my position at the housing program was going to be cut in a few months, I approached the committee with the idea that I commit my time to leading the launch of JAC. They were on board, and one of the organizations represented on the steering committee reallocated some grant funds to support JAC in its first six months of development.

I wrote to Judith and the other founders of PAC, letting them know we were going to forge ahead, checking to see if they had any concerns or wanted to get involved, and asking for their well wishes. Judith wrote, "So glad to know, slowly but surely, others—including you—have been working toward developing the vision we started with quite a few years ago. . . . I send tons of support and gratitude that you've built PAC into what it is now and that you're going to take it to the next level."

It's been two and a half years since I left the predictability and relative comfort of a nine-to-five position and took the terrifying leap into founding a national nonprofit organization. It's been a wild ride, that's for sure, but I believe Judith would be really proud of what's been accomplished.

JAC has become a thriving national network that includes nearly four hundred incarcerated artists and just as many people outside of prison who are committed to our mission.

This includes incarcerated artists' loved ones, teaching artists, formerly incarcerated artists, students, activists, and so many others.

We've developed numerous ways of connecting people inside and outside of prison with opportunities to connect with and learn from one another. I think what might excite Judith the most, though, is the number of young people involved with JAC. In years past, "veteran" teaching artists working in prisons worried there would be nobody to receive the torch. I can say for sure this is not going to be an issue. Over the course of the last year and a half, JAC has hosted over thirty college-age interns, many of whom become so immersed in our work that they choose to remain on the team for multiple terms.

The culture we've created within JAC embraces authentic presence, collaboration, and vulnerability—the ideals Judith held tightly to. At JAC, emotions are never too much. All of "you" is welcome here. We nurture and nourish one another, allowing our hearts and values to drive everything we do.

JAC has been and continues to be shaped by—and belongs to—all of us: the artists who so courageously entrust us with their creative work and stories; loved ones advocating for and standing by their imprisoned friends, family members, and partners; volunteers who help ensure that every piece of mail from artists in prison receives a personal response; interns from across the country and beyond who've shown up fully for one another through Zoom and worked tirelessly together to carry JAC through a global pandemic; every teaching artist, previously incarcerated artist, student, activist, and curious community member who has brought their wisdom, truth, and creativity to our weekly online Network Gatherings, Create + Connect workshops, to our first National Convening, Art for a New Future (we felt you there with us, Judith!), and to their pen pals through our arts-based correspondence program, the pARTner Project.

Together, we're actively creating the world we want to live in, one in which everyone can experience a sense of belonging, purpose, and meaning, and modeling a vision of justice that embodies healing, connectedness, and care, rather than punishment, separation, and retribution.

Crossing Paths with Judith

Joseph Lea

On June 14, 2015, in an email response to Judith, who had written to wish me well on my pending retirement from the Connecticut Department of Correction, I reiterated her hope that our paths would cross many more times. When I wrote those words, I expected that to mean a physical crossing of paths—that we'd attend a prison arts conference together, or I would be in California and we'd have lunch, or that she'd publish a book of her poetry or art and I'd attend a reading. I never considered any other way for our paths to cross.

After her passing, I started to think about those good intentions to see Judith again. I regretted not making that happen sooner. I still regret not having seen her again, but our friendship spanned nearly two decades, and during that time we saw each other only a handful of times.

A physical reunion wasn't necessary. We stayed in touch mostly by email and always over a shared interest. She was always there any time I undertook a new project and often offered candid feedback whenever I reached out (and even when I didn't). We sent people to each other whenever someone was in touch about working in prisons on either coast. I was amazed at her intricate level of connections to those doing interesting work and her ability to put people together.

* * *

I first crossed paths with Judith in 2004, after she wrote to author Wally Lamb following publication of *Couldn't Keep It to Myself.* This was an anthology of women's writing based on a group he had led at York Correctional Institution in Niantic, Connecti-

cut, where I also taught. Judith had asked to visit the writing
program the next time she was in New York City. I wasn't part
of the program, but I was interested in any of the arts happen-
ing at York. When she eventually arrived, I was struck by her
kind and inquisitive nature. I read her memoir *Disguised as a Poem*
for the first time and found it to be an eye-opening experience
about what it took to create art in prison. I regularly shared *Dis-
guised* with anyone interested in offering an art project at York. It
was written like a teaching manual for prison art practitioners.
I have since reread it countless times. Each time I find something
new and grow a bit closer to Judith.

In my blurb for *By Heart,* I called it "a remarkable memoir
of two powerful personalities brought together through poetry
and prison. Through Judith's genuineness a poet awoke and
found a way to live a fuller life in spite of confinement, and
through Spoon's honesty and talent many people will be com-
pelled to contribute to society, even if society has abandoned
them." That was true then and it is even truer today.

I remember spending time with Judith in Philadelphia in
2007–2008, where several York teachers attended a prison arts
conference hosted by the Mural Arts Program. It was my first
time at such an event, but Judith was well known and deeply
entrenched in the prison art scene. She made the rounds like an
old soul. It was at this conference that the Prison Arts Coalition
was formed, which is now the Justice Arts Coalition. Judith was
a founder and an active member. It's part of her legacy.

Over the years, we stayed in touch. In 2010, I was able to see
Judith in person when Buzz Alexander held a gathering to cele-
brate PCAP (Prison Creative Arts Project) in Michigan. That
year, I was also busy rereading *Disguised as a Poem* to prepare for
my first time teaching a college course. Judith was just starting
to do book talks for *By Heart,* and she held one at the University
of Michigan while we were at PCAP. She had a stack of mailing

labels with Spoon's signature to adhere them to the books she was signing. She asked me to take pictures so she could send them to Spoon. She wanted him to see the response to their memoir. It was another way Judith took care of people, making sure even though Spoon couldn't be there, we'd still feel his presence and he would know about it, too.

* * *

Since her passing, I have mourned the loss of Judith as a friend and colleague in all the traditional ways. I have looked through her poetry and collages, I've reread old emails, and I have even braved teaching from *Disguised as a Poem* and *By Heart* this year in my class at Trinity College in Hartford, as it helps humanize the issue of mass incarceration for my human rights students. I wasn't sure how all of this would feel. There was sadness but also a sense that our paths were crossing again, as I had hoped. Not physically but no less deeply.

When Spoon wrote a wonderful tribute to Judith, which was published on the Justice Arts Coalition's website, I reached out to him. I had heard so much about Spoon over the years from Judith but had never spoken to him. We have talked and started to get to know each other. Even after her passing, Judith is still bringing people together.

Spoon has twice visited my Zoom class on Human Rights Through Performance via a prepaid cell phone link. He has also taken part in the class of a colleague who teaches Art and Social Justice at the Royal Conservatoire of Scotland. In my class, Spoon shared his poetry and answered questions. As he spoke, I'd remember images from *Disguised as a Poem* of how he waited on the stairwell at San Quentin for Judith to arrive for their poetry class. I'd recall learning about their meeting in class and her innate ability to offer people the space they needed to find themselves and their talents.

Judith was a great teacher, and I can see signs of her in Spoon. Judith's writing also shared her giving nature, her vulnerabilities, and her mantras, like reciting the prayer of Saint Francis each time she arrived at San Quentin. I listened to radio interviews with them about *By Heart* and their love of poetry and each other. In the preface to their memoir, Judith recalls how Spoon would say, only partially in jest, that in introducing him to poetry she had saved his life. Thus, she was forever responsible for the life she had saved. She did not feel responsible for Spoon, she wrote, but, rather, to him, and all the other students behind bars. In that reflection, I heard my friend and colleague talking about what was most important to her, and being responsible to others and letting them grow.

Fortunately, Judith left us a full record of her thoughts, talents, interests, and advice in the form of interviews, books, art, and shared letters. I can only imagine her home, its walls pinned with quotes that she knew would inspire and help her and others. Each year at Christmas, I remember receiving a quote printed on a piece of paper in an envelope, which always seemed poignant. I wish I had kept all those quotes in a book or shoe box, but that is not what I do. I keep them in my heart and revisit them whenever I think about Judith.

* * *

To honor Judith's life and work, I established an annual award for a first-time entrant in poetry through Koestler Arts, a prison arts charity in the United Kingdom. At my request, the recipient also receives one of Judith books. This was my attempt to send Judith's name, work, and words as far as I could so that her impact would continue to be felt even if she is no longer physically with us.

In 2020, the inaugural award was given anonymously to a poem called "Fresh Air and Forgiveness." It emerged from a writing group at HMP Dumfries, an institution for young offenders in Scotland. I think Judith would have especially appreciated the two final stanzas, which appear below. She was determined to see people in all their complexity, and believed fervently in the redemptive power of nature:

> How easy in life it is to look and not see?
> To feel trapped, restricted and dehumanized.
>> But even here we can be transported beyond.
> Let the wind blow away labels that negatively define you.
> Allow the natural shower to wash you clean.
>
> Breathe in the fresh air.
>> Feel the warmth of the sun.
>> It's a basic human right, entitled to all.
> Exhale and breathe deep.
> Fresh air and forgiveness is free to you!

⋆ ⋆ ⋆

Grieving doesn't end, but we do eventually move forward. Through the award, and the memories, Judith and I continue to cross paths.

From Student to Shepherd

Tiffany Golden

I didn't know Judith Tannenbaum.

I learned about her not even a year after she passed, when I was nominated for the 2020 Judith Tannenbaum Teaching Artist Fellowship through the organization I work with, Chapter 510 & the Dept. of Make Believe.

What I do know about Judith is that she found teaching meaningful and wanted to empower others to teach well. I feel a strong connection to Judith as a teaching artist who writes. Teaching is a unique career, one where it is easy to give all you have for those in your care. Writing requires time to nurture your voice. Learning self-care is a necessary tool for the survival of any teaching artist and practicing writer. It is something that I am still learning.

In early 1999, I had a life crisis. I suffered a deep depression. I attempted suicide. I am thankful that I survived that crisis.

This is a letter to that younger me.

* * *

Dear Tiffany,

You think you have failed. You haven't.

You think you have nothing to contribute. You do.

I know life doesn't seem clear right now; you are overwhelmed with pain that you thought would easily resolve if you faced it. Here's what I can tell you: I understand the depths of the despair you feel. I also know who you are. You are resilient. You are going to make it through this tough time, even though it doesn't seem like it.

Soon you will try something new. You will embark on a new journey.

You will teach.

Teach what?

Filmmaking
Cooking
Poetry writing
Instrument making
Collage
Art
Creative writing
Nutrition
Mindfulness
Songwriting
Reading
Science

I know you are wondering how you can teach most of the things on that list. Easy. You keep learning. You keep growing. You never give up. Sure, you have meltdowns and battle depression, and cry a lot, but here's one thing that you do: You choose to keep growing.

Soon, you will get the space you need to look at what pains you. You will breathe. You will teach a class. That class will change your life. You will shift from student to shepherd. Souls will be in your care. Impressionable souls. Hurting souls. Kind souls. Brave souls. Beautiful souls. They will grow to trust you. They will grow to love you. And you will trust them. You will love them. They will make you learn to problem-solve on your feet. They will teach you to dig a little deeper, to ask, "What's really going on with you?" They will make you know the importance of seeing people, believing in people, and believing in yourself.

Will teaching be easy? Good God, no. But it will teach you patience with others, and yourself. It will teach you that people can come back from mistakes and try again. That you can try again. Because you will try again. With every lesson you teach, you will get a chance for your heart to heal and open a little bit more. You will see the brilliance in others. Their divine light. You will see them struggling. And though you will not always be able to take away their pain, you will be able to sit with them. And like you, they will get through it.

You will be nicknamed "Ms. Tee" by one of your students, and it will remind you of Grampi calling you "Big Tee," and you will love it. Because teaching will feel like home. Teaching allows for the community and connection you crave. And even though your first time will feel like a disaster, you will get better at it.

It will bring you joy. It will bring you peace.

It will let you love and be loved.

You are meant to teach, Tiffany Golden. Hang in there; you have much life to live.

With love,

Future Ms. Tee

Notes

Preface

1. Judith Tannenbaum and Spoon Jackson, *By Heart: Poetry, Prison, and Two Lives* (Oakland, CA: New Village Press, 2010), 73.

Unfinished Conversations

1. Judith Tannenbaum, "Way Out in the Bay," *Carve This Body into Your Home* (El Cerrito, CA: Nehama Press, 2012), 28.

2. Ibid.

3. Ibid.

4. Wendell Berry, "Manifesto: Mad Farmer Liberation Front" in *New Collected Poems* (Berkeley: Counterpoint Press, 2013), [TK].

Looking and Listening

1. Jacqueline Jones Royster, "When the First Voice You Hear is Not Your Own," *College Composition and Communication* 47 (1996): 1, 29–40, https://doi.org/10.2307/358272.

2. Judith Tannenbaum, *Disguised as a Poem: My Years Teaching Poetry at San Quentin* (Boston: Northeastern University Press, 2000), xi.

3. Ibid.

4. Nazim Hikmet, "Some Advice to Those Who Will Serve Time in Prison," in *Poems of Nazim Hikmet.* (New York: Persea Books, 1994), www.perseabooks.com.

5. Tannenbaum, *Disguised as a Poem, My Years Teaching Poetry at San Quentin* 19–20.

6. Ibid., 20.

7. Ibid., xx.

8. Susan Sontag, *Regarding the Pain of Others* (New York, Farrar, Straus and Giroux, 2003).

9. Ibid., 72.

10. Spoon Jackson and Judith Tannenbaum, *By Heart: Poetry, Prison and Two Lives* (Oakland, CA: New Village Press, 2010), 192.

11. Tannenbaum, *Disguised as a Poem: My Years Teaching Poetry at San Quentin*, 49.

12. Ibid., 149–150.

13. Ibid., 150.

14. Ibid., 150–151.

15. Ibid., 151.

16. Spoon Jackson, "Speaking in Poems," *Teaching Artist Journal* 5 (2007): 1, 23, https://www.tandfonlinecom/ doi/abs/10.1080/15411790709336712.

17. Ibid., 4.

18. Ibid., 59.

19. Daniel Karpowitz, *College in Prison: Reading in an Age of Mass Incarceration* (New Brunswick, NJ: Rutgers University Press, 2017), 25.

20. Tannenbaum, *Disguised as a Poem*, 119.

21. Judith Tannenbaum, "Introduction," *North Coast Correctional Facility: A Nouvella* (California Department of Corrections, 1989).

22. Tannenbaum, *North Coast Correctional Facility*, 49.

23. Ibid., 64–66.

24. Ibid., 66–67.

25. Ibid., 54.

Legacy

1. Judith Tannenbaum, "Human Beings Together," *Turning Wheel*, Summer 2002, 26–27.

Permissions and Credits

Wendell Berry, excerpt from "Manifesto: Mad Farmer Liberation Front" from *New Collected Poems*. Copyright © 1973 by Wendell Berry. Reprinted with the permission of the Permissions Company, LLC on behalf of Counterpoint Press, counterpointpress.com.

Elmo Chattman, Jr. "Disguised as a Poem." Reprinted with permission of the Estate of Elmo Chattman, Jr.

Nazim Hikmet, excerpt from "Some Advice to Those Who Will Serve Time in Prison," translated by Randy Blasing and Mutlu Konuk, from *Poems of Nazim Hikmet*. Copyright © 1994, 2002 by Randy Blasing and Mutlu Konuk. Reprinted by permission of Persea Books, Inc. (New York), www.perseabooks.com. All rights reserved.

Spoon Jackson and Judith Tannenbaum, excerpts from *By Heart: Poetry, Prison, and Two Lives*. Copyright © 2010 by New Village Press. Reprinted with permission of New Village Press.

Judith Tannenbaum, excerpts from *Carve This Body into Your Home*. Copyright © 2012 by Judith Tannenbaum. Reprinted with permission of the Estate of Judith Tannenbaum.

Judith Tannenbaum, excerpts from *North Coast Correctional Facility: A Nouvella, California Department of Corrections*. Copyright © 1989 by Judith Tannenbaum.

Judith Tannenbaum, excerpts from "Looking at Looking: 33 Glimpses," an unpublished manuscript. Reprinted with permission of the Estate of Judith Tannenbaum.

About the Editors

SARA PRESS is Judith Tannenbaum's daughter. She grew up to the sounds of the typewriter and witnessed how her mother developed deep relationships with so many and shared her convictions about teaching, writing, and social justice.

MARK FOSS is a Montreal-based author whose works include the novels *Molly O* and *Spoilers,* as well as essays and creative nonfiction. He became friends with Spoon Jackson following work on the production of *Spoon,* a film by Michka Saäl, completed in 2015.

SPOON JACKSON is a poet serving a life sentence without the possibility of parole in California state prisons. It was Judith Tannenbaum, through her poetry classes in San Quentin State Prison, who introduced Spoon to the power of words. Indeed, Judith edited and published Spoon's collection of poems *Longer Ago.* In addition to his own extensive list of publications, Spoon also coauthored a memoir with Judith, *By Heart: Poetry, Prison, and Two Lives,* published by New Village Press in 2010.

About the Contributors

KATIE ADAMS is a senior lecturer in the Department of English, Appalachian State University, Boone, North Carolina.

NEELANJANA BANERJEE's writing has appeared in *Harper's Bazaar, Prairie Schooner, PANK Magazine, The Rumpus, World Literature Today,* and many other publications. She is the managing editor of Kaya Press, an independent publishing house dedicated to Asian Pacific American literature, and teaches writing at UCLA.

JIM CARLSON was the artist facilitator and program administrator for the California Department of Corrections and Rehabilitation between 1984 and 2014. He continues to be active in providing arts programming to men at Mule Creek State Prison.

The late **ELMO CHATTMAN, JR.**, was incarcerated for thirty-three years within the California State Prison System. During his years at San Quentin, he was a student of Judith Tannenbaum. Elmo was a published poet, short story writer, and served as a reporter and then editor of the *San Quentin News.*

BILL CLEVELAND is an author, musician, and filmmaker, and he also directs the Center for the Study of Art & Community, working to advance art as a change agent in communities and social institutions. Bill's podcast, *Change the Story/Change the World,* can be found at https://change-the-story-chan.captivate.fm/listen.

KATE DOUGHERTY taught poetry in schools on the coast of Northern California and is the author of *The Elk Poems.*

MARK DOWIE is an investigative historian and journalist based outside Point Reyes Station, California. He is the award-winning author of several books, including *Losing Ground: American Environmentalism at the Close of the Twentieth Century* and *Conservation Refugees: The Hundred-Year Conflict Between Global Conservation and Native Peoples.* His magazine articles have won nineteen journalism awards, including four National Magazine Awards.

AMY FRIEDMAN, an author and creative writing teacher, is the cofounder of POPS the Club, which cultivates an inclusive space for California youth who have been stigmatized and silenced by their experiences with the carceral system.

J. RUTH GENDLER is the author of three books that include her art: *The Book of Qualities, Changing Light,* and *Notes on the Need for Beauty.* She has taught writing and art to children and adults in a variety of formats and settings for over thirty years and has exhibited her art nationally.

TIFFANY GOLDEN is a teaching artist for Chapter 510 & the Dept. of Make Believe in Oakland, California. The inaugural recipient of the Judith Tannenbaum Teaching Artist Fellowship, she writes children's and middle-grade books focusing on the joy and magic of childhood.

ARACELY GONZALEZ was a teaching artist for WriterCorps, which teaches creative writing to more than five hundred at-risk children in San Francisco each year.

JANET HELLER is a poet, teacher, and community arts activist in Oakland. She founded the San Francisco WritersCorps and Chapter 510 & the Dept. of Make Believe. In partnership with Mesa Refuge, Janet created the Judith Tannenbaum Teaching Artist Fellowship to provide time and space to write for Oakland teaching artists.

ALLIE HOREVITZ is a clinical social worker based in the Bay Area of California. Along with Judith Tannenbaum and others, she is one of the founders of the Prison Arts Coalition, precursor to the Justice Arts Coalition. Allie has been involved in prisoners' rights advocacy through her work with the Prison Law Office and the Habeas Corpus Resource Center.

ROSELI ILANO has more than a decade of experience as a community organizer and educator, with an emphasis on using storytelling to bring people together. She is a WritersCorps teaching artist alum and worked at WritersCorps with Judith Tannenbaum from 2011 to 2014.

SPOON JACKSON is a poet serving a life sentence without possibility of parole. He is the author of numerous works, including the poetry collection *Longer Ago,* which was edited and published by Judith Tannenbaum. He and Judith cowrote the memoir *By Heart: Poetry, Prison, and Two Lives.*

WENDY JASON is founding director of the Justice Arts Coalition (JAC), based in Silver Spring, Maryland. Her twenty-five-year career in social services and many relationships with those most directly impacted by incarceration brought Wendy face-to-face with the myriad ways in which the carceral system perpetuates harm on an individual, communal, and societal level. She now combines her background in restorative practices, mental health, and education with her passion for the arts to foster vibrant, inclusive, and nurturing communities that model and promote social justice and collective care.

LEAH JOKI is an actor, writer, director, and teaching artist. She has taught and/or performed in more than thirty prisons. She was an institutional artist facilitator for fourteen years and the first female to run an arts program in a men's maximum-security prison in California.

DEVORAH MAJOR is an award-winning poet and fiction writer, creative nonfiction writer, performance artist, editor, and part-time senior adjunct professor at California College of the Arts, in San Francisco. A former poet in residence of the Fine Arts Museums of San Francisco, she was also the city's third poet laureate.

ANNA PLEMONS was a creative writing teacher in the California Arts in Corrections program from 2009 to 2019. Her book, *Beyond Progress in the Prison Classroom: Options and Opportunities,* chronicles that work. She is currently the associate vice chancellor for Academic and Student Affairs at Washington State University Tri-Cities, in Richland, Washington.

LUIS J. RODRIGUEZ is a poet and writer with sixteen books in all genres, including the best-selling memoir *Always Running, La Vida Loca, Gang Days in L.A.* From 2014 to 2016, Luis served as the poet laureate of Los Angeles.

BARBARA SCHAEFER is an interdisciplinary artist whose paintings and photographs are exhibited internationally. She has taught at the WritersCorp program in the Bronx, and her work has been published in *Days I Moved Through Ordinary Sounds: The Teachers of WritersCorps in Poetry and Prose.*

TENESHA SMITH, known as Tenesha the Wordsmith, is a poet, musician, performance artist, and special education teacher. Her most recent spoken word album, *Peacocks & Other Savage Beasts,* explores the intersection of identity, culture, trauma, and love.

MAW SHEIN WIN's second full-length poetry collection, *Storage Unit for the Spirit House* (Omnidawn, 2020), was long-listed for the 2021 PEN America Open Book Award. She often collaborates with visual artists, musicians, and other writers, and is a 2021 ARC Poetry Fellow at UC Berkeley.

MARNA L WOLAK is a National Board–certified bilingual (Spanish) teacher/literacy coach at Sanchez Elementary School, San Francisco Unified School District, and an adjunct professor in the Teacher Education Department at the University of San Francisco.

BOSTON WOODARD is a writer, musician, literacy tutor, event organizer, and prisoners' rights advocate. He is the author of *Inside the Broken California Prison System* (Humble Press, 2011).

FURY YOUNG is a multidisciplinary artist and activist from the Lower East Side of New York City. His work includes music, film, poetry, and collage. He is the founder and executive director of Die Jim Crow Records, a nonprofit record label for formerly and currently incarcerated musicians.

Judith Tannenbaum (San Quentin in the background)
Credit: Rainer Komers.

About Judith Tannenbaum

JUDITH TANNENBAUM (1947–2019) was an educator, poet, writer, and speaker. She shared and taught poetry in schools and community centers, and was faculty with WritersCorps, a highly respected project that placed professional writers in community settings to teach creative writing to youth. Tannenbaum found a passion for prison justice and reform after teaching at San Quentin State Prison through the California Arts Council and the California Department of Corrections and Rehabilitation. She continued to give poetry workshops and performances in prisons and juvenile facilities nationally. Her memoir *Disguised as a Poem: My Years Teaching Poetry at San Quentin* (Northeastern University Press, 2000) is considered essential reading for anyone wishing to teach art in prisons. Through her work at San Quentin, Tannenbaum fostered a 20-year-long friendship with poet Spoon Jackson, and the two recounted their lives and experiences in the double memoir, *By Heart: Poetry, Prison, and Two Lives* (New Village Press, 2010).

THE JUDITH TANNENBAUM TEACHING ARTIST FELLOWSHIP honors an Oakland teaching artist with a writer's residency at The Mesa Refuge in Point Reyes, CA. In partnership with Chapter 510, Oakland's youth writing center, the annual fellowship provides an opportunity for a writer who has made a significant impact in the lives of youth.